Just Do One Thing

SINGLE
THREADING

The art of doing more
by doing less

Dylan Monaghan

Host of the 555 am Show

You are NOT your brain!

Executive function (You)

35 bits processed by You

11 million bits processed by Brain

ISBN 978-1-961513-02-0 Hardcover
ISBN 978-1-961513-01-3 Paperback
ISBN 978-1-961513-00-6 EPub
ISBN 978-0-9986082-9-7 PDF

Names and identifying details have been changed to protect the privacy of individuals.
Author: Dylan Monaghan
Cover Design: Erik Suswanto

First Published 2023, 2024   4th Edition

Dylan's Books
1100 Bellevue Way Ste 8A #860
Bellevue, WA 98004

an imprint of DRCJ Books

FOREWORD

"You hold the power to multiply goodness."

- Ambassador Tomeo RD M Gressard

I met Dylan on a trip to Osaka, Japan. During that journey, we exchanged ideas on human potential. We discussed the path to achieving higher states of existence through changing the way you think about the world and your daily environment.

We really do create the world that we believe exists. If you change your belief, instantly the world around changes to match your new belief.

Until you experience this shift, it is difficult to imagine. After you experience the shift, you want everyone to have the same opportunity.

And as you share these secrets, you discover how many minds are locked against this simple secret.

In this book, Dylan shares a simpler path to unlock the secrets to experience this higher level of existence.

Dylan really captures the spirit of the Journey with his fresh new take.

Explore with Dylan as he unravels the secrets to reaching your peak potential. He will show you how to coax your brain into cooperating and producing the remarkable results you desire.

The world is waiting to see you shine, and it begins with mastering the art of doing more by doing less.

If you are holding this book, please read it to the end. Then come back and review. Take notes in the margins. You can even contact Dylan for more details.

Include SingleThreading in your life.

Dylan is a guiding light in this transformative journey. Rise above the ordinary and become extraordinary.

Foreword

Dylan enthusiasitcally shared how you can embrace your own unique perspective while opening your mind to possibilities that lie ahead.

SingleThreading for success is your path.

The time to transform is now.

The journey to become the best version of yourself begins here.

I enjoy SingleThreading and use it everyday. You can too.

Ambassador Tomeo R.D. M-Gressard
Chairman, Marine Foundation Trust

Do things you find easy,
but looks like **work**
to others.

Begin with
THE END
in mind

CHAPTER 1 — ONE THING

You get better at the things you spend time doing.

We've lost something. In our drive to become well-rounded, we have learned to avoid specialization. Have you noticed a generation of lost souls wondering what they are good at? We survived high school, college, and more. Somewhere during our education we forgot to focus.

Becoming well-rounded has killed our productivity. The happiest among us are doing what they love, while the rest of us are wallowing in well roundedness.

Realize you are a uniquely powerful force in the universe. There is a mission waiting for you. When will you start?

When will I start? That thought started this book.

When was I going to launch my mission? I am so busy doing whatever it is I am busy doing. But I'm not doing the One Thing I have been put on the planet to do.

What about you? Are you are busy living your life, while not living the life you were destined to live?

From February 2021 until February 2023, I held a live radio show at 5:55 am. I broadcast via the Clubhouse drop-in audio App to people around the world.

We had free-flowing conversation with new topics every day. We built bonds of friendship between our regulars, and newcomers.

One of our signature conversations was the idea of doing less to achieve more. We called this "The One Thing Discussion." Everyone agreed we were happiest when we focused on the things we loved to do.

Some of us were uncertain what our One Thing might be. Many were busy living with no time to focus on their One Thing. I was busy guiding the discussions, believing I was focusing on my One Thing, when in fact, I was stuck.

I was living in the past, sharing fun stories of other people's lives. I was not living. I was not creating new memories.

I told everyone to "Do ONE Thing!" while running dozens of parallel projects.

It was the trap of "Do as I say, not as I do".

You could see me following the siren's song as a willing participant at events without creating a future. I was multitasking my days.

Where did my goals go? Why did I have a blank slate? As work projects came along, I worked diligently on them, but I didn't have hobbies.

February 2023 I unplugged from Clubhouse to focus on my full-time job. I continued working, attending meetings, and visiting customers. I dropped out of activities not related to work. I spent time on me, pausing for self-reflection. I did not unplug and sit on a mountain waiting for spiritual wisdom but I stopped "hanging out."

I counted: we work 8 hours a day with an hour for lunch. Add an hour commute each way and that's 11 hours we give to someone else.

It requires 55 hours to work the 40-hour work week. If we sleep 6-8 hours a night and spend 1-2 hours engaged for breakfast and dinner, that's 42-56 hours for sleep and 7-14 hours for food. We get 3-4 hours a day for ourselves.

We want to socialize, meet friends and family, entertain and relax. We need time to exercise; time to organize and time to create.

Our time on earth is limited. We are exhausted and need an escape. So we invented the vacation—a week or ten-day diversion from our daily routine followed immediately by returning to the daily grind.

Looking through a bigger lens, we have 80 summers

and 80 winters in our life. How many summers have you "spent" already? More than 50 of mine are behind me.

I took a step back during those few private hours I had each day to look at what I was doing.

If I didn't get started doing the work I was put here for, my life would end with a list of regrets. This book is a journey of things I realized.

I hope these simple insights bring benefit to your life.

Find your way to do your One Thing. Hold onto your passion! If you lost your mojo, let's get it back.

Remember the most precious thing in your life **is your time and your attention. Every minute is important.** Your attention determines the value of your time.

Focus on your One Thing today.

Delayed Gratification Produces Results

find small
rewards along
the journey

CHAPTER 2 - TIME FOR CHANGE

I am not the master. I cannot teach you.
I can only show you how to learn.
You are responsible for your learning.

Wonderful moments from our past survive like trophies on the mantle—forgotten, dusty, and untouched. When today rolls around, we have forgotten the hard work that brought us those memories.

Creating new, special memories takes time and energy. In our normal day-to-day life, we stay in our groove and avoid unnecessary expenditure of energy. We want to coast and enjoy our days.

Or do we? Do we really want to coast as a passenger in life? Wouldn't you prefer to live your days filled with joy? Does that joy appear out of reach?

Let's try a different approach. Can we accomplish more by doing less? Can we focus on things that make a difference in our life and result in joy?

Focusing on One Thing is better than doing busy tasks that fill up time and produce no long-lasting joy.

To follow the more rewarding path something must change. We must change. If we make the same decision we get the same result. That's guaranteed.

Anyone who has accomplished something changed in some way. They changed their mind and they changed their actions. Small changes are sufficient.

Being raised in a poor environment is a drag on your future ability, but it is not a permanent condition. Being born with benefits is a boon to your future, but this too is not a permanent condition.

Start today; commit to finding the best path forward. Commit to learning what to change, how to change, and when to do it. You must take this first step.

It takes 3 minutes or less to make the decision to change. From the instant you decide to make a change, you embark on a journey that did not exist

3 minutes ago. New thoughts change the world.

The answer to the question when should I change, is now. This is obvious. You have the power within you to change and you already know what needs to change.

In the pages that follow let's talk about what and how.

A note to you: read and re-read these pages. Take a moment. Stop, think, and read again. Take your time. Over time, you will (re)discover concepts that might have eluded you before.

Write in the margins. Underline concepts that resonate. Add your own thoughts. This is your living document. Share your ideas. Email me with your ideas: dylan.monaghan@gmail.com.

Your brain traps you in a past that you cannot change, it ignores the promise of a bright future, and it fumbles actions we should be taking now, in the present moment.

Everything you ever did; you did in a "now and

present" moment of that day and time. There is no other way. We are linear beings living in a time dimension with one direction. You cannot execute tomorrow's plan until tomorrow arrives.

By the same logic, you cannot return to yesterday to make adjustments. When you worry about a future that has not arrived you waste the potential of now.

We are happiest when we live fully in the moment. Worry fades away and you have access to your peak performance.

I have the magic formula to achieve any goal. Let's permeate your "now" with meaning and happiness. Join us.

Let me fill your life with meaning and happiness. Join the SingleThreading Movement. The pages that follow contain the magic formula you need for success.

CHAPTER 3 – SINGLETHREADING

Upgrade your mind.

Remove the obstacles you invented
Find the Path.

The word SingleThreading means to sew using a single thread that is not doubled. SingleThreading is also used to describe the way early computers processed their instruction code, one process thread at a time; sequentially.

These days, computers process instructions in parallel using multi-threading.

As a computer geek and Electrical Engineer by training, and Computer Programmer by family association, I grew up watching my father in a giant computer room sitting in front of the IBM 360 writing code.

It was a massive machine that filled a room, with the thermostat set so low it felt like icicles might drip down from the tables. That machine was revolutionary, upgradable, and only did One Thing at a time. It was a Single Thread machine.

I like the way this word sums up working on One Thing. It reminds me of a simpler time when we did One Thing well and finished it before moving on to the next.

It is fun to talk about the multitasking we use to survive and the ton of things we get done at once, but it is NOT the path to success. Multitasking is great for simple activities when the outcome is not critical yet both tasks need to be finished.

I can watch a movie while eating dinner. I can clean the house while I listen to a podcast or watch the news. I can send emails during a Zoom meeting.

We can split our attention between tasks, but we won't do either well. It gives us the sense we are accomplishing a lot in a little time. But for genuine success, we need results that multitasking cannot achieve.

Important, creative tasks require the full power of your brain. It is better to use your entire mind focused on a single topic.

Hyper focus generates results. Multitasking kills your productivity and your reduces your happiness.

When we focus on One Thing until we finish, we unlock the secrets to achieving more: more happiness, more results, more success. This is the SingleThreading Movement.

Let's share our goals and strategies. Together we can do more than we can do alone.

It might be difficult. It takes practice, dedication, and a willingness to work diligently to eliminate distractions and increase productivity.

Even now, I am thinking about weeding the lawn instead of writing this chapter. I want to watch something cool on YouTube (of course I will call it "research"). I need to do laundry. However, I will stay focused and finish writing this chapter. Goals.

Make this commitment with me. Today, we

prioritize our time to focus on what matters. We will no longer waste time on activities that don't contribute to my goals. We are working to enjoy today, now. We will not postpone joy.

This is a daily struggle. When I forget to focus, I check my SingleThreading Calendar to get back on track.

During the process of focusing and SingleThreading we will rediscover our spark and regain our sense of purpose. We see our goals by engaging them. Together, let's identify your SingleThreading focus and purposefully achieve our goals.

This book is our journey and my commitment to you. Be inspired to join the SingleThreading movement. Discover the power that brings focus to your life.

CHAPTER 4 – YOU ARE NOT YOUR BRAIN

You must learn a new way to think before you can master a new way to be.
—Marianne Williamson

There are two of you reading this page. You and your brain. But who is in charge right now? Is it You or is it your brain?

"You" are the logical, planning, energetic version of yourself. This "You" sits in your frontal lobe and is fully developed around age 24. This is your Executive Function.

The other you is your hidden brain. The core. The Lizard Brain—the amygdala, a tiny almond- size gland at the center of your brain that combines inputs from the world around you, and feeds the final answer to You without explanation.

It has been around since you were an infant. It is like a 3-year-old permanently living inside your mind watching everything you do.

Unfortunately, if we do not recognize there are two centers in the brain, the stronger amygdala will usually win the argument about what you should do next.

This is the source of road rage, jealousy, lack of desire to do anything, difficulty when trying to keep a diet, etc.

These days with always-on social media frenzy buzzing around our input sensors (eyes and ears), our brain's Executive Function goes into passive mode.

When the Executive Function is not given challenges to solve, it reduces in size and atrophies. This makes the hidden brain and the amygdala grow stronger in relation to the Executive Function and we feel stressed, unfulfilled, and experience a dull sensation about our life in general .

Feeling depressed? Depression starts and resides in the amygdala. This is often the little voice of doubt. This is the part of you that stops you from using your gift.

Allowing the amygdala to direct your actions is like driving down the highway without touching the steering wheel. The car will be fine until it loses balance and then it could dart off the road at any moment.

Learning to exercise restraint over the hidden, Lizard Brain requires practice. It is not automatic.

Mindfulness training works. Practicing Yoga and listening to your own breathing works.

Your Executive Function can only focus on One Thing at a time.

Anytime you feel distracted, you must hand control back to the Executive Function and quiet the amygdala.

Through repeated and regular training of putting the Executive Function in control, the frontal lobe literally grows larger and stronger. It becomes easier to control the 3-year-old in your mind.

You cannot be successful until you comprehend the true power of your complete brain. You are already a complete package. You have the talent, the drive, the awareness, and the vision to live your life fully.

All the answers we ever need are already inside each of us. We only need to learn how to listen to ourselves without the noise of the fussy 3-year-old amygdala fueled hidden brain.

When we find our purpose, we are happy from within, with no need for external accolades. There is a purpose for every person on earth. There is no need to struggle needlessly searching for your purpose when it is already written inside your mind.

The brain is a complicated organ, but it is always changing thanks to neuroplasticity. If you treat it well, feed it properly and give it the right nutrients, it will help you reach your best self.

You <u>can</u> change and you can learn new things.

CHAPTER 5 – TO MULTITASK OR NOT

Don't be afraid to fail.
You are not failing.
You are learning.

In our modern, digital world, multitasking is normal—it's almost required. We are not living the simple life of our ancestors. Life competes for our attention. We do everything at once because everything comes at us all at once. I know firsthand. You do too.

Are you multitasking right now? I am and I am the author of a book on how not to multi-task. I am typing emails, sending texts, checking YouTube and trying to find some good music.

But I enjoy the ability to do these things. I'm not willing to trade places with the society of 100 years ago. I like my modern digital gadgets. Even though research says that multitasking is bad for productivity, memory, and mental health, I still do it.

Multitasking is when we do more than One Thing at the same time.

We believe multitasking is an efficient and effective way to do more in less time. That's why we do it. But when we multitask we are not actually doing multiple things at the same time; we are switching our attention from one task to another.

That switching is not free. There is a cost to switching your attention between different activities. It's a tax on your brain for not focusing on One Thing.

If your autonomous system does one of the tasks (like walking) we don't divert much cognitive attention. However, when we talk on the phone while perhaps driving a car, we take away cognitive energy from the primary task (driving) to switch our brain to the secondary task of talking. It doesn't matter if you are hands free or not. Anytime we multitask, we risk cognitive overload. We are slowing down our progress and decreasing productivity and safety.

We are living in an age where distracted drivers are testing the limits of the safety features on our modern cars. 8% of fatal car accidents resulted from distracted driving. The National Highway Transportation and Safety Administration (NHTSA) says that distracted driving causes 3,000 deaths per year and 300,000 injuries from distracted driving. This is completely preventable!

Stanford University demonstrated the impact of distractions in a study on multitasking. They asked participants a series of questions to measure their working memory. Task-switching experiments showed light and heavy multitaskers had less capacity in their short-term memory. They were distracted and had difficulty focusing. The single-taskers were resilient in the face of distractions: they had more working memory and stayed on task longer with less effort.

Constant distraction is terrible for our productivity. Smartphones and digital devices are always in our hands or on our wrists or resting on the table within sight. It's too easy to become distracted.

The University of California Irvine (UCI) tells us it takes 23 minutes to get our focus back after a distraction. That's nuts. That means most of us have never regained focus.

We are constantly in a state of distraction. If I don't get notifications, I check my phone to see if it is still on and connected. I have a fear of missing a notification! (FOMAN)

This decreases our productivity, and also ruins our mental health. A University of British Columbia study says when you are interrupted by notifications throughout your day, you experience higher levels of stress and anxiety than people who do not get notifications and who finish their tasks.

The writing is on the wall but we don't see it because we are busy watching our smartphones, tablets, TVs and other screens that appear constantly in front of us.

The brain loves new, so every time something appears on a screen, the brain eagerly replaces the boredom of sameness with exciting news from our digital devices. So we feed the brain the shiny attention that it wants.

This constant barrage of "new" comes at the cost of reduced memory capacity. You are not imagining it. We remember fewer details of our life due to the constant inputs.

The University of California San Francisco (UCSF) observed that young people could handle heavy media multitasking better and could return to their original task with less negative effects than older people. As we age, it seems our working memory and the ability to switch tasks diminishes. The older we get, the effects of multitasking get worse.

In other words, multitasking is bad if you want a fulfilling life with better outcomes. It gets worse if you continue to multitask as you grow older.

What can we do? Let's look at fictional characters: Bob and Mia.

Bob is a busy person who runs around doing one thing after another. He is not making much progress on his big project.

Mia, on the other hand is chill. She is focused, relaxed, and gets things done. She does not appear "busy" even though she works diligently.

Bob's day starts early in the morning. After hitting snooze a few times on his alarm, he rolls out of bed and rushes to work. He skips breakfast and grabs a cup of coffee as he rushes out the door. Some days he is stuck in the drive-through line at Starbucks on his way to work.

When he gets to his desk, he is bombarded with emails, phone calls, and meetings he forgot about. He barely catches his breath before he's on to the next thing.

Bob feels like he is on the back of a firetruck, constantly putting out fires. He is not making progress on his big project because he is busy taking care of other people's projects.

Mia, on the other hand, wakes up before her alarm goes off and has a plan for her day. She drinks a tall glass of water, takes time for meditation, stretching, and yoga before checking her phone.

Over a warm cup of relaxing tea, she looks down at her phone to see what is new. Now she reflects quietly on her goals for the day. She is using the SingleThreading One Thing calendar and knows her priorities and plans her tasks accordingly. She focuses on one task at a time and takes scheduled breaks to recharge.

At work, Mia is focused and efficient. She doesn't allow distractions like social media notifications to enter her day. Her phone automatically enters do-not-disturb mode based on her location. She says no to requests that don't align with her priorities. She works steadily throughout the day and makes progress on her big project.

At the end of the day, Bob is exhausted and feels like he's been running in circles. He hasn't accomplished much on his big project and feels frustrated.

Mia, on the other hand, is satisfied with her day's work. She's made significant progress on her project and is looking forward to tackling more tomorrow.

Would it surprise you if I told you that I am both Bob and Mia? Both of these lifestyles have been me at one time. I am not always Bob nor can I stay like Mia. The results are clear though. I prefer being "Mia." I am more often like "Bob."

We are all probably more often like Bob. While we secretly want to be like Mia, we outwardly despise her. Although we want to be like her, with our schedule and our time demands we revert to Bob. Mia rarely becomes our reality.

So what is the difference between Bob and Mia? Is it ever possible for Bob to become more in control like Mia?

We can see that Mia understands the importance of focus and prioritization. She knows she can't do everything at once. She knows she has to focus to achieve her best results. She wants quality results, not scattered results.

Bob is juggling too many things. The result is that

he is frazzled and not a lot gets done.

Bob knows intellectually that being busy doesn't equate to being productive. He knows that being too busy will hinder his productivity. But, like most of us, he doesn't know how to stop being busy. He doesn't know how to say no to meetings, requests, or the ding from social media.

The statistics and studies on the negative impacts of multitasking and constant distraction paint a clear picture: Focusing on doing a single task is a more effective path to getting things done.

You might want to do everything at once. Your brain loves to respond immediately to new things when it can be a spectator.

That being said, you are human and there is no way to be perfectly 100% efficient all the time. The goal is to identify the big goals and the path to completion.

We have to reset and figure out our true priority.

Do Your Best
Until You Know Better

when you know better, do better!

CHAPTER 6 – TIME AND PLACE

I've always been in the right place and time. Of course, I steered myself there. —Bob Hope

B ob and Mia were fictional characters from the previous chapter. We have a little of Bob and Mia in ourselves. We can reach that Mia-state even if Bob is lurking to jump out any minute.

How can we act more like Mia?

The key is to find the time and place for Bob and Mia to coexist in your life. It would be unwise for you to drop everything you are working on suddenly to focus on only One Thing.

If you take on too much change at once, you are likely to revert to old methods and claim that you were not cut out for this concept. Don't quit on your One Thing so fast.

There is another path.

Look at what you want to accomplish, set aside time for it, and focus like a banshee on SingleThreading. Not everything. Just the things you know will make a difference. I suggest starting with 15 minutes a day. Appendix 1 talks about how the 3x5 system can help you.

For now, I want to talk about Time and Place. When should you SingleThread and when is it okay to multitask?

Here are a few examples to get you thinking.

Absolutely turn off the notifications on your phone when driving a car or operating machinery. You can set this up to automatically turn off notifications when it senses you are driving. Do not multitask when you are moving down the road. Make driving a priority. Go cold turkey. Focus on driving. Make this a golden rule.

During your mornings, be like Mia. Do not touch the phone first thing. Start an alternate daily routine. Find things you must do before touching your phone. Or, if you absolutely must touch the phone, set a timer for 3 minutes. Then start your alternate routine. Give the phone a break.

For a month, do not take your phone out when you are on the toilet. Finish your business without the phone. Focus on understanding your body. Yes, I just recommended that you start SingleThreading your poop sessions!

Throughout the rest of your day, find or create blocks of time to focus on finishing your projects. Minimize distractions and focus on one task at a time during those blocks so you can improve your SingleThreading muscles.

For the rest of your day, after you have identified the areas that are off limits to multitasking, build other fences around the things that you decide are OK to multitask. Don't be a Scrooge and insist on 100% compliance—give yourself areas to play.

Some acceptable study-backed examples of good multitasking are:

Listening to music while exercising has a positive effect on our mood. It helps with motivation, making it easier to push through those times when you feel fatigued and don't want to finish your workout.

Listening to the same workout tape each time will keep your motivation high. Your Brain will recall the routine as it recalls the song that is playing. The Brain wants a suitable conclusion and will subtly push you to finish the music as planned. This may be from the release of dopamine in the brain which enhances feelings of pleasure.

The dopamine hit comes from anticipating the workout, not from the act of working out. The music is like Pavlov's bell. It tells your mind that a big event is coming! That is your reward.

Doodling or drawing while listening to a lecture helps you focus and retain information! This is because the brain processes new information by combining inputs.

By writing, you move your hand. The signal in your brain to create the motion of your hand is tied to listening. The two inputs combine to give the brain a stronger signal when you need the information later.

Processing more than one input at the same time is also useful when learning a new language. When you combine two actions: listening while reading text; writing while listening; reading written words; etc., the different processing centers—visual and auditory—or visual and motor activity fire neurons at the same time; one enhances the other.

Doing low-stress tasks such as folding laundry or doing the dishes while talking with a friend on the phone, is a good example of multitasking. You could listen to a podcast or catch up on your Netflix. It can help you feel more relaxed and connected. We think this is due to oxytocin; the hormone associated with social bonding and feelings of well-being.

Multitasking works well when we consider the task, the time and place, and when we make a conscious decision on whether it is appropriate.

Multitasking should be avoided when completing complex and mentally demanding tasks that require focus and concentration. We need to be fully present and focused when we are driving, taking care of patients, talking to our customers or our boss.

We should probably not be checking social media when we are out at a social event having dinner with friends. Sometimes we have to remind ourselves of the proper priority.

CHAPTER 7 – RISKY BUSINESS?

Where there is no struggle, there is no strength.
—Oprah Winfrey

We have seen that engaging in multitasking behaviors hurts our productivity. It might even be detrimental to our safety. But we still do it. Again and again. Our hidden brain doesn't care about our safety as long as it's desires are satisfied. This book will not change that.

Because of the complexity of desire, there is no single explanation that captures why we do risky multitasking like texting while driving. The hidden brain tricks us into doing things that intellectually are bad for us and rationalizes why we did it after the fact. The brain will get what it wants. Getting its desire will satisfy the brain.

The only option is to program the hidden brain

for an alternate purpose. When the hidden brain is busy and engaged, it doesn't even think about multitasking.

Imagine a horse jockey in the middle of a race trying to talk on the phone. The race is over in minutes. The level of intensity of the race makes such a thought unimaginable (except in a comedy skit).

If you pre-program your hidden brain not to participate in these risky behaviors, you can develop new patterns that will restrict your bad behaviors and enhance the good habits.

You are not limited to the existing programming that exists in your hidden brain. You are limitless and this ability to reprogram is the reason the brain can change if you decide to change it. You have the capacity. You can re-write the code.

Our hidden brain has full autonomous control over what we do and doesn't always tell us why it did what it did. Your brain processes life in real time. We rationalize our behavior after the fact, and that gets us in trouble. We say things contrary to our true nature. Because the brain wants to protect itself in that moment.

The first step to getting around this problem is to be aware of the fallibility of your brain.

Understanding that "You are not your brain" is the key to SingleThreading. In order to learn to make the best of your time, we must separate the concept of you from your brain.

But how does the hidden brain take over?

Dopamine reward system: This is the reward system that the hidden brain loves to get more of. We check our phone the second we hear that ding. Switching between tasks when multitasking does the same thing. The dopamine hit reinforces the behavior even when not in our best interest. Look out for this.

In any instance of time, the hidden brain absorbs 11 million bits of information. But our conscious mind (Executive Function) can only absorb about 40-50 bits of information in that same instant. And our conscious focus is limited to a single thing at any one time.

So, our hidden brain can absorb more than we realize and can be tricked into deciding based on things we have not been conscious of. Intuition falls into this category. And subliminal messages do too.

The brain's ability to focus attention is limited and can be tricked and overwhelmed. When we are bored, our brain sends the attention off to find some other stimuli. These days, that often means checking email or social media. The brain wants something new to enjoy.

We are creatures of habit: We do things predictably. Habits are hard to break. When you try a new way, it is difficult, uncomfortable, and even if it is better, you revert to tried-and-true methods. I struggled to use ten-key* input for Japanese on my smart phone. I was accustomed to Romaji** input. Eventually I persisted and got pretty good, but it was an uphill struggle to replace the habit.

Ten-key is a method of character entry based

on the telephone keypad of numbers 0-9. Each key is assigned five characters in the Japanese language based on pushing the key once for the first character, or "flicked" up/down/left/right for the other 4 character options.

**(Romaji input uses the English alphabet on a QWERTY keyboard to phonetically input Japanese characters). Ten-key is faster.

Multitasking is a habit: Even when you know it is dangerous or unproductive, it's hard to stop.

Habits are formed through repeated behavior. You will never eliminate it from your brain. You can only create a new habit. It takes time for the new habit to become your new, preferred method. It is easier to never form the bad habit than to correct it.

If you have to make a correction, start now, and be relentless. Old habit patterns are always ready to be reactivated, so be vigilant.

Overconfidence bias: We overestimate our ability to multi-task successfully. We underestimate the risks associated with performing multiple activities simultaneously.

This overconfidence bias leads us to believe we are invincible when in fact, we are flawed and easily duped. The evidence is clear; we cannot handle multiple tasks at once.

Even if you think you are special and are convinced you can handle multiple tasks, the evidence suggests otherwise.

Executive Function deficits: Executive functions, such as working memory and cognitive control, are critical for planning, decision-making, and controlling impulsive behaviors.

When you are young (younger than 24 years old) your Executive Functions are still developing. You know right from wrong, and yet might do the wrong thing anyway. You may even surprise yourself!

Same goes for anyone under the influence of alcohol. You think you can drive fine. You believe you are in control. But it is a lie. Your Executive Function has been impaired by the alcohol and you no longer have sound judgement.

So, you need guard rails in advance. If you know you are going to drink, don't drive. Know that in advance.

If you are going into a meeting where you routinely text, leave your phone at your desk.

If you multitask when you should not, adjust the environment so that you cannot.

For your morning routine, buy an alarm clock and use it instead of your phone. Place your phone far from your bed. Put it in the living room if you can!

If your Executive Function is taking a break and not controlling the body, you may be prone to multitasking and other risky behaviors.

Brain plasticity: The brain is a highly adaptive organ and can develop new neural connections with new experiences. You can learn a new language. You can also get out of the multitasking habit.

Give your Brain the experience of SingleThreading

so that it can learn to enjoy that state of flow that comes from being fully engaged in One Thing. Disengage from always multitasking to help rewire your brain for better behavior.

Fear of missing out (FOMO): This goes back to that dopamine hit. When your hidden brain realizes it has not had a dopamine hit, it will knock on your Executive Function (EF) door and ask for some more.

The fastest hit is usually a quick scroll through social media; a visit to your latest breaking news site; or a little video from YouTube or Netflix. The Internet age makes it easier than ever for the Brain to grab an update from the endless stream of online information.

The fear of missing out on important information or social events motivates our brain to seek information. When we locate bits of information, the brain sends back a positive reinforcement congratulating us for the multitask.

In fact, we probably could have waited. We probably

should have waited. We do not need to be plugged in so often.

Time pressure: Sometimes, we feel pressured to complete tasks in a limited amount of time. Often we insist we must do everything at once and we multi-task. Scammers tap into this.

Re-evaluate. Could you get more time? Which task is more important? Could you divide the time and work sequentially on each task for a fixed amount of time? Does everything absolutely have to be done now? Are you being pressured by a scammer?

What if you eliminated some tasks from the list and did them later? Multiple tasks within a limited time frame are a recipe for disaster. What if you asked for more time?

Before you accept the time pressure, check what you can do to relieve the pressure.

Mind-wandering: The default mode network (DMN) is a set of brain regions that are active when the brain is engaged in passive tasks.

Anytime we are not focused on a cognitive task, our mind enters this highly active state. Even though you are not actively thinking about a project, the hidden brain is at work organizing thoughts, sifting through old memories, daydreaming, or just drifting.

The DMN activity level quiets down when you are active and doing something. If you are constantly multitasking, the DMN never has time to fire up. If you actively pick up your cell phone and start scrolling, your brain does not have time to operate the way it normally should.

Modern life is full of distractions. Demands on our attention never seem to end.

Whenever we feel overwhelmed, we should probably dial back our multitasking habit, back away from alcohol, and dig into some mindful meditation and reflection.

Plan downtime when you have nothing planned. Do not schedule every minute of your day. Do not overload the brain. It is very sensitive.

Do not let the hidden brain drive your decisions. Put that brain in park and restore your Executive Function to control your conscious self.

It's not your fault that you multi-task when you shouldn't. You are human.

Learn how to regain control of your whole brain.

Energy invested *IN YOU,*
changes the world

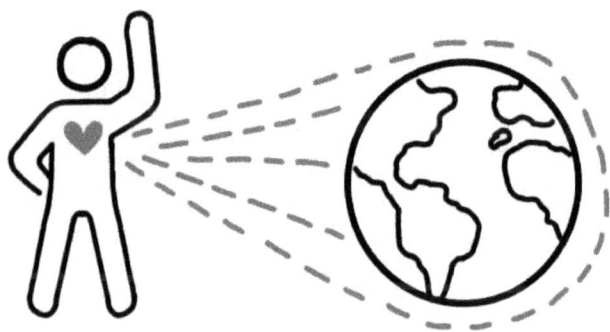

CHAPTER 8 – LIFE-LEVEL MULTITASKING

Time is a created thing.
To say 'I don't have time'
is to say 'I don't want to.' —Laozi

We talked about the basic level of multitasking: task level. When we spend our days operating at the task level, we never reach the strategic, life level.

To make big strides, we must elevate our thoughts above the task level and operate at the strategic level. Which career path to follow and what to do with our life.

Open your mind to this discussion and learn how to make better decisions.

When we multitask at the task level and ignore our strategic level, the Universe is unsure what to send us to ensure success. The Universe is here to help you achieve success (or failure). Good luck and bad luck are options for us to choose from. Either choice is within our grasp.

If you simultaneously attempt to publish three books, build a course (or two), run a radio show, perform in a band, and do this while holding down a regular day job (and maybe drive Uber on the weekends), the Universe does not know where you want to succeed. The results are mediocre everywhere.

Maybe the reason you are doing all those side hustles is to see which one will hit pay dirt. You are not sure, so you hedge your bets. You are following the old adage about having multiple streams of income.

Whatever the reason, you are not doubling down on your One Thing. Either from lack of time, lack of understanding yourself, or maybe a lack of understanding about the world.

The Universe is ready to provide everything you need, but only One Thing at a time. Even if the Universe simultaneously sent you everything you need for all your side projects, you probably would not be capable of handling the load.

That is why I want you to focus. If you focus on One Thing, you will be more aware of the conditions that are right for your next move. You will pick up on details you might otherwise miss. We are wired to discover the things that we seek. I call this "looking for red".

LOOKING FOR RED

Looking for red is a simple test you can use to better understand your hidden brain.

Take a few seconds right now to look around. Count everything that is red. Any shade you consider red is acceptable. You do not have to remember what it is, only the number of red items you counted.

Finished counting?

Okay, now, stop looking around. From memory and without looking, how many green things did you see? Did you get a good count? Look around now. Does green seem to pop more than before? Do you see more green than you remember seeing while "looking for red"?

That's what happens when looking for red. Your Executive programmed your hidden brain to ignore everything that wasn not red. It only "sees" red things because you asked it to.

This is how our brains work. It can only find what we send it to fetch. If you focus on your One Thing, you find it. If you focus on bad luck or bad timing, you will have it.

If you ask the Universe for everything or too many things, you will never see what you want from the full bounty that is available. It will be there, mixed in with everything contained in the universe. You will be too absorbed and distracted to detect the patterns.

There will be too many competing bits of information. The important information will be muddled together with unimportant information.

It's easy to find a tennis ball in a stack of needles. Even when it's buried, you will identify the telltale hump.

It's hard to find a needle in a stack of needles. You will waste your time. It's going to be impossible to achieve success. The odds are stacked against you.

Someone not familiar with how luck operates might call the person looking for the tennis ball "lucky" while the other one looking for the needle is "unlucky".

I say that you decide your luck. The decisions you make in life define your luck.

If you decide you must have a specific and special needle from the stack of needles, while I decide I need the tennis ball from the same stack; my search will be over in seconds, while you will still be hunting long after.

If you don't know that you can look for tennis balls, you might not even notice the tennis ball in that stack. You first need an active interest in tennis balls.

When you run around from one big task to the next, with no focus, you don't reap the rewards of completing a task. You will be the person searching for needles in a stack of needles. You never get that big break. You will be stuck looking for the wrong thing in the wrong place.

Let's try a different approach.

Imagine I ask you to drive three cars 100 miles. The three cars are parked together at the same starting location. You will get paid for delivering each car after it arrives at the destination.

You might want the three cars to arrive at the same time. You could fall into the trap of starting the drive for one car, traveling a mile, getting out, and running back to the second car. You drive that second one a bit then run back for the third car. You are running as fast as you can between cars and driving as fast as you can. It takes forever to cover the 100 miles. You focused on the wrong details.

New day, same problem, you put your thinking cap on and decide to bring a scooter or bicycle with you. You speed up the transfer time between the cars. You are playing a game of leapfrog.

Anyone who tries this approach realizes that running back and forth takes more time than driving. This is the price of switching.

What if you drove car #1 the entire 100 miles in one trip. You will figure out how to get cars #2 and #3 later. After payment for the delivery of the first car, you think of ways to return to the starting line to get the other cars.

You could walk back, ride your bicycle/scooter. You could take a bus or an Uber. You could fly back.

Once again at the start line, you could drive car #2 and get that second payment. Lather, Rinse, Repeat.

Maybe you could use your 1st payment to hire another driver or two.

Maybe this metaphor is your life. Are you running back and forth between cars and don't realize it?

By thinking smarter and elevating your thinking, you realize it makes more sense to focus your energies on One Thing to completion.

By adopting a strategic mindset, your productivity increases. Now you waste less time and come out with genuine achievement.

You can have this right now. Stop running from project to project. Do not hire yourself out to solve everyone's problems. Solve your own first. Do not do everything because you are talented.

Perhaps you have heard of the famous basketball player Michael Jordan. He is of course known for his achievements in basketball.

Jordan won six championships with the Chicago Bulls, had five MVP awards, and if I understood basketball better, I would share more of his amazing statistics. Jordan is one of the greatest basketball players of all time.

He was even a two-time Olympic medalist winning Gold Medals in the 1992 and 1984 summer Olympics.

Did you know he also dabbled in baseball and golf?

Jordan played in the minor leagues for the Birmingham Barons, a Double-A affiliate of the

Chicago White Sox, during the 1994 season. He played in 127 games, batting .202 with 3 home runs, 51 RBI, and 30 stolen bases. Wow.

He did not play pro golf, but he played in celebrity and pro-am tournaments. He claimed his best score was a 68 at the Bear's Club in Florida.

While his baseball and golf game were impressive, His comparative advantage was in basketball.

Even if he got better at golf, 68 is not enough to develop a career at the top of that sport.

In other words, he was great at other sports, but he *excelle*⟩ at basketball and he went all in. He dabbled in baseball but basketball brought him greater success.

What if Jordan spent his time multitasking baseball, basketball, and golf? What if he got his real estate license during the championship games as a backup plan in case he lost a game or two? What was his Plan B? Sounds ridiculous, doesn't it?

What about Warren Buffett? Buffet was one of

the most successful investors of all time. What did he do differently? The gurus tell us to spread our investments into multiple industries to reduce risk and hedge our bets. But Buffett had a different approach.

Instead of making numerous investments across all industries, he focused on specific companies in fields he understood. He researched the market and the decision makers. He picked companies that were discounted or overvalued using these insights. His sweet spot was companies with a strong competitive edge that were undervalued.

Power generation plants with predictable earnings won his interest. Looking back at his holdings, we see he focused on insurance, banking, and consumer goods.

He did initially invest in airlines because he finds them fascinating. But now, he now avoids them because he believes the models are too complex to predict. They may have strong performance, a competitive advantage and good leaders, but with their up and down cycles driven by consumer behavior, the price of oil and a dozen other factors, they are not the kind of company that Buffet will invest in anymore. Even Buffett can learn from his experience.

We see Buffett is focused on long-term returns. He looks for high-quality companies that he believes will grow and perform well over time. He is not looking for an overnight success. By focusing on select companies, he gains an understanding of the market. He makes informed decisions. He is SingleThreading his investments!

No book would be complete without mentioning Steve Jobs on his return to Apple computer in 1997. The company was struggling financially because they were competing across a wide range of products. This story encapsulates the key message of this book: Do less to achieve more.

Jobs simplified the product lineup at Apple by removing peripheral products like printers, scanners, and digital cameras. These were outside Apple's core business. By dumping the non-core products, the company could focus on its core strengths of making high-quality computers.

Internally, Jobs was opposed vehemently. He faced stiff opposition to the reduction in items but he believed focusing on high-quality products would help Apple succeed. His focus saved Apple.

Jobs narrowed Apple's products to desktop computers, laptop computers, displays, and software. He believed these core areas would allow Apple to differ from the competition and stand out.

Jobs concept was a "digital hub." The Macintosh computer became the central device for managing and organizing digital content like music, photos, and videos.

The vision was simple but required energy to execute. What was Job's Plan B? Did he spend nights and weekends working on his CPA degree?

That's a ridiculous idea, right? He focused on the core products at Apple.

What about you? Are you focusing on the big project that will make a difference in your life? Or are you building Plan B? Are you splitting your time among different plans? Perhaps you have a Plan A, B and C. That's what the pundits tell you to do. Invest in a safe strategy; have a fallback plan.

I did the same thing. I have a day job that I love and it pays the bills. To finish this book, I gave up having fun on weekends and evenings. "Being boring now" to have a better life later. If I cannot help myself first, how can I help anyone else?

Before writing this book, I was spreading myself like peanut butter across a range of Plan A, Plan B, and more. I was Mr. Fixit and Mr. CanDo. I said yes to every opportunity and created additional projects on my own. I helped everyone who asked and even a few people who did not. I was busy.

My projects were exciting but only a few got finished. Other projects were in a perpetual state of incompletion. (They still are). It is easy to start something new. It's easy to quit. It's easy to jump to new things. Continuing what you have started is harder. Continuing to a final conclusion has a better outcome.

There is a time and place for multitasking. "Be intentional". Decide where you will not multitask. Write these down so you don't forget.

Set time to find your big project and then spend all your time working on it. You will reap the rewards of that focused time.

CHAPTER 9 – TROUBLE FOCUSING

*All problems become smaller when you confront
them instead of dodging them.*
—William F. Halsey

If you have trouble focusing, assess your current habits and routines and identify what is hindering your ability to focus.

Maybe your inability to focus comes from a common distraction that we have—the presence of other people. Whether it's coworkers stopping by for a chat, family members interrupting us while we're working from home, or friends wanting to catch up, other people can be a significant distraction.

We need social contact. We are social creatures. But when it is time to create we need a shift in thinking. A shjift in thinking is best accomplished in a distraction-free environment.

It might be a quiet space to work, turning off

notifications on your phone, or using noise-canceling headphones to block out the world around you. Even with no music, the reduction in noise can increase your focus.

Find that quiet place and ensure you prepare everything you need in advance. Avoid the urges to walk away to "find something."

It should be the right temperature, the right lighting for you and not physically challenging. Comfortable, but not comfortable enough to fall asleep. Set the table and chair at the right height for your work. Consider a standing table. Help keep your fragile attention from breaking down.

A lack of motivation or lack of interest in a task can make it challenging to focus on that One Thing. When we're not interested in what we're doing, it's easy to get distracted and lose focus.

Try turning it into a game. One point for every minute you stay focused on the task. Track your points and shoot for a high score everyday. I use the Atracker app ($4.99 at the time of this writing).

In today's world, distractions are everywhere. Whether it's social media notifications, emails, phone calls, or the chatter of coworkers, distractions can make it difficult to focus on the task at hand.

Recognizing and eliminating distractions is crucial for achieving productivity and reaching our goals:

If you have a lot to do, find the One Thing that will make your efforts today worthwhile. "Eat that Frog" is a great book that describes the goal of finishing the big task first. Everything after that is gravy.

Do that one task first and don't stop until it is done. Do your other smaller tasks after. Avoid switching between tasks so that the important task gets done.

If you are struggling to get to the next step maybe you need a break. Taking regular breaks helps to reset and refresh your mind. Make it every 50 minutes or every 90 minutes. Take a short walk, do some stretches, or perhaps perform some deep breathing exercises to help clear your mind.

If you are too antsy to stay put even for 50 minutes,

try 3 minutes. See if you can make that 5 minutes. Keep extending the time.

I cannot focus, I will use a timer to keep me in my seat. When I am overly focused, I use a timer to remind me to take breaks. Use the focus mode on your phone to turn off distractions and hide the troublesome apps. You don't have to count on willpower if you plan ahead.

Want to reset your brain? Practice mindfulness. (I love this.)

Mindfulness practices include yoga, meditation, deep breathing, and following ancient rituals. These things work! If you have not found the one that works for you, my guess is you haven't focused on one.

It is a lot like restarting your computer. It clears out the memory circuits that got congested. If you practice 15 minues a day that's about 7 hours a month. Stay with it for at least these 7 hours before you can determine what works for you.

If you want to avoid the trap of no motivation, plan your day the night before. If you forgot to plan last night, the second best time is now. Build a plan for the week. Check it daily and you will know if you are ahead or behind. Use the SingleThreading One Thing planner for best results.

Finally, be sure that you are getting enough regular sleep. I have irregular sleep habits which make it hard to get a good night's sleep. I cannot count on feeling tired, so I must take extra precautions to prevent staying up all night. Find what works for you and be loyal to your sleep. Don't cheat. Your brain needs a certain amount of sleep to ensure you are at your peak efficiency when you are awake.

To have a life-level plan, you need to focus. Then, build on that plan every day. A little at a time, but every day.

While you are focused on a task, turn off your phone or set it to do not disturb. The American Psychological Association found that brief interruptions, like answering an email or taking a call, can bring your productivity down by 40%.

Your brain hangs on to bits of data that you added when you spoke on the phone keeping you from returning fully to the work that was interrupted.

If you want to get the maximum benefit from focusing but cannot seem to start, try to set a maximum of 3 minutes to work on the problem or project. If you can trick your brain to get started with the promise of 3 minutes. You may find that the brain, once started on a path, likes to continue.

If you can stay with it for 15-30 uninterrupted minutes, you may enter that wonderful state of Flow and can continue for hours unabated.

I like to work in cafés because there is no laundry to fold, no dishes to wash, and nothing for me to be distracted by other than people.

And to avoid being distracted by people, I put on noise-canceling headphones. I don't even have any music on half the time. It takes too long to select music. And if I enter a flow state, I don't even notice that I have been without music!

It only takes a few minutes to decide. But it takes a lifetime to execute. So be careful what you choose to do. It will have consequences. If you identify the things that distract you, you can win this game. Stay in it to win it.

Let's get SingleThreading today!

Stop inventing Obstacles

Find The Path

FAIL Faster!

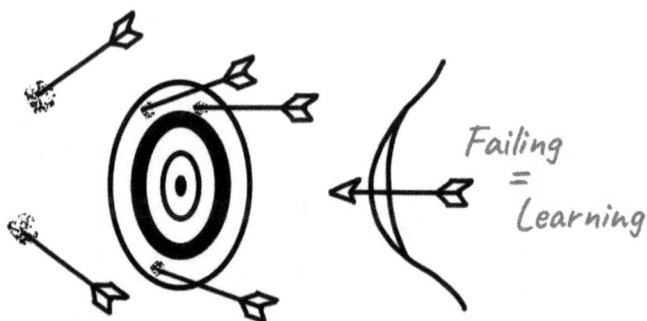

Failing
=
Learning

Fail Faster = Learn Faster

CHAPTER 10 – FINDING YOUR GOAL

You already know what to do.

Some of us are lucky to find our calling and to live a life fully immersed in it. The rest of us work so that we can make enough money to do the things we really want to do. Many of us seem to be trapped in a cycle of making money to pay bills with nothing else filling our days.

How do we find our mission in life? Without knowing what fulfills us, without a powerful experience driving us toward or away from something, most of us go through life without experiencing the intense spark of finding our purpose.

Finding our goal in life is a challenging and ongoing process. To really understand yourself well enough to achieve a connection with the universe that opens you up to your purpose, requires self-reflection, introspection, and an open mind.

Sometimes the simplest observation is the best. My favorite story is called "Acres of Diamonds" told by Russell Conwell, the founder of Temple University.

Russell Conwell was an American Baptist minister born in 1843 in Massachusetts. He spent most of his life traveling and giving speeches on religion, politics and personal success.

He believed that education was the key to success. Russell wanted an affordable school of higher education to make education accessible for all.

He encouraged his audience to look for practical opportunities to improve their current life to*ay. He stressed hard work and perseverance combined with your own innate talents and resources.

He believed that to reach your fullest potential, you must live in harmony with your existence. "Acres of Diamonds" is his most famous speech with a book of the same title.

Russell describes a farmer who sells his land and sets off to travel the world in search of an acre of diamonds that he was prophesied to find. The farmer spends his entire lifetime searching the world and never finds the acres of diamonds he was promised.

Meanwhile, the new owner of the farmer's land notices an odd spring in the middle of the farmer's field covered by a board. Removing the board, the new owner discovered something shiny. This was the largest diamond mine discovered to date. The farmer's prophesied diamonds were under his feet from the beginning.

Russell used this story to inspire his audiences to look within themselves and their current circumstances for their success and purpose.

Your purpose in life is already in your mind. It is so obvious that you may take it for granted because it is easy for you to do.

Many of us believe that if it is easy for us to do, it must not be valuable to others. We make the mistake of using mirroring, the concept of projecting our abilities, values, and expectations, onto other people.

If you are struggling to understand your own purpose in life. Think about where you spend most of your time, or most of your money.

Look at your passions and interests. What do you enjoy doing? What do you naturally gravitate toward? What is fulfilling?

If nothing comes to mind, what do you get compliments on? What about you fascinates others.

You can also look at things you dislike. Do you dislike cleaning? Is exercise something that you avoid? Often, the thing we avoid contains a hint of important opportunities for us. When we truly dislike something, we often have deeper insights than someone who enjoys it. Others may also dislike this and your insights might solve others' problems too.

I don't like memorizing numbers, so I find clever connections to make it easy to do complicated math. I did the same with Japansese and now I can help others.

What about your strengths and skills? What are the things that you are good at, and that come easily to you? Consider how you can use these strengths and skills to make a difference in the world. If you can make art quickly and effortlessly, you can reach a quantity of scale that no one else can match.

Think and reflect on your values and beliefs. What is important to you? Russell felt strongly about education for all. He started a university that is well renown worldwide. Consider the impact you have made in the world. What do you want to continue? How would you like to grow the positive impact on your legacy?

Still stuck? Why not create a list of potential goals? Write all the ideas that come to mind, no matter how big or small. Don't worry about whether they seem realistic, just get everything down on paper.

Prioritize your list. Look at each idea and consider whether it aligns with your passions, skills, and values. Prioritize the ideas that feel most meaningful to you.

Warren Buffett, the world's most famous investor, is widely quoted after he encouraged his pilot, Mike Flint, to identify his key goals by asking him to make a list of his top 25 career goals.

He then asked the pilot to circle the top five goals that were most important to him. Buffett further asked the pilot to focus only on those top five goals and to ignore the rest. He was insistent that even a little attention on the bottom 20 goals was a waste of energy that should be given to the top five, and only the top five.

Here, we talk about SingleThreading to bring laser focus to one goal at a time to really achieve success.

FIND YOUR GOAL

The 80/20 Rule: After you list your goals, look at the top 20% of those goals that will have the most impact on your life. Usually 20% of our efforts produce 80% of our success in life. This means that if we can focus on the 20%, we are more likely to experience increased success. That's where our energy should go.

Mind Mapping: Great apps abound, but I like using pen and paper. This is a wonderful visual process. Starting with yourself, draw each thought that comes to mind and how it is connected to your other thoughts. Keep the pen moving and expanding your understanding of yourself. This visual map will contain hints of all your potential goals.

Look for themes on this map to realize what drives you. Have you been avoiding the themes that seem to draw you in or push you away?

Need more help? Make a chart with a SWOT Analysis: Evaluate your potential goals by considering your strengths, weaknesses, opportunities, and threats.

Use this analysis to identify the goals that are most feasible for you to implement. Look at your strengths as a possible place to start a successful transition. Look at your weakness as something you could develop a project around.

Do not only consider the things you feel others will enjoy, consider that you will be the one doing it. If it does not resonate with your own soul, you will run out of energy when things get difficult.

Finding your goal in life requires self-reflection, introspection, and an open mind.

Everyone of us has a purpose. We are born with that seed planted within each of us, constantly driving us toward our purpose.

We seem to push away from our purpose because we prefer to believe society, the latest fad, or what our friends and parents might expect from us. We are social creatures and want to be accepted by the people around us.

I ask you to open your mind to really explore your passions, strengths, and values, and create a list of your potential goals.

The process of finding your purpose is ongoing,

and it's okay to revise your goals and priorities as you grow and change.

When you commit yourself to your mission, the people you need to support you will appear. And they might not be the same people around you today.

It begins with your first step.

Share your goal with me at our online SingleThreading community.

Plan Your Year in Advance!

Plan

Track Your Plan!

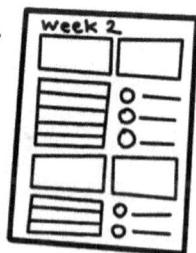

week 2

JANUARY

What you measure will improve!

CHAPTER 11 – PLANNING YOUR YEAR

If you fail to plan. You are planning to fail.
—Benjamin Franklin

Some days, I forget that this moment in time is really important. Right now. This second. This minute. This hour.

Conceptually, I know that time is passing. And I know I need to make the most of each moment. But when the moment is here, I find it hard to focus.

It turns out that our hidden brain cannot understand time. We can estimate time, we can observe time, we can see days and months on a calendar, but we do not know time.

Your hidden brain does not know how old it is. Your Executive Function can do math from your birthdate, but if no one told you, and if you did not count how many summers have gone by, you would not know your own age.

Our hidden brain always thinks we will have more time in the future. If we are busy today, we make plans for the future, because somehow we think the future will be less hectic.

Our bodies are trapped in a fixed stream of time. We cannot jump around from one point in time to another. We can travel in time, but always in one direction, and always at the same general speed.

But our brain and our perception of time changes from moment to moment. We experience time in our own way. For kids, Christmas never seems to come soon enough. For adults, we can barely remember the drive home from work.

Albert Einstein proved that time is relative. If you travel fast enough, your time reference will change and time will be slower for you, relative to me.

If you jump into a super-fast spaceship, take a trip for 8 years at or near the speed of light, and come back as quickly as you can, you will have aged exactly 8 of your years. Back on earth, I may have experienced 50 years during that same time.

You will only notice the difference when you return and make a comparison to the things you left behind.

When we discuss how far away something is on earth, we use meters, miles, or kilometers. In Tokyo, you might substitute those measures of distance with a measure of time. It takes about 40 minutes from Shinjuku Station to Haneda Airport.

Within our solar system, we describe distance in the minutes it takes light to travel. For reference, a photon moves at the speed of light: 299,792, 458 meters per second, or 186,000 miles per second.

If you shoot a single photon around our planet earth, it would take 0.13 seconds to make the trip. It takes 1.3 seconds for light to reach us from the moon. 8 minutes from the sun. Jupiter is between 35-52 minutes away.

To talk about enormous distances in the universe, like the distance to stars and other galaxies, we measure the distance in light years—the distance that light travels in a year. On this galactic scale, light is not particularly fast.

Alpha Centauri A and B are "only" 4.367 light years away. There are 160 galaxies that are within 100 million light years from earth.

Those places are far away. Alpha Centauri would require 6,000 years to reach using the technology we have today.

We can see the light from those far away galaxies here on earth. When you look up at the stars or use a telescope, the photon that enters your eye departed that location 3.5 billion light years ago. You are seeing the past.

Now, for the mind-bending, mind-blowing concept.

Imagine a photon traveling from a galaxy 3.5 billion light years away—the photon that sped through the galaxy for those billions of light years to reach you—do you know how long the trip, at light speed, would take for the photon in terms of time?

Remember, this is from the photon's point of view. How long is the trip?

0 seconds. That's right. The photon does not experience time at all. The instant the photon is created, it is in your eye.

When someone asks you if something can move faster than the speed of light, it is a trick question. From the perspective of the photon, time does not exist! Theoretically, if you could eliminate your mass, you too could travel at the speed of light.

Perspective matters.

Let's bring this discussion back to you and your brain.

Without a comparison, time has no meaning. We can track the sun rising and setting to compare days. We can track shadows across the ground to compare hours and minutes. But absent external signals, humans lose track of time. That is why we need some system to aid our brain in keeping on track to achieve our goals.

What is the best way to plan out a full year?

When I think about a big goal, I overestimate what I can do in an hour or a week, while I underestimate how much I can accomplish in a year.

Whether it is writing a book or learning a new language, most of us fall into these categories.

We assume we can do more in the coming week, while failing to recognize how a little effort now can reap big rewards in the future.

So it is important to start with a big goal for the year. Instead of a new year's resolution, let's create a new year SingleThreading plan.

One of the simplest ways to build a plan is to deconstruct from a single idea.

The year is 365 days long. If you tried to make a plan that started on day 1, and then day by day you added a task, you might find that you run out of ideas of things to schedule, or by the final day of the year, your tasks are all stuck in the weeds as tactical moves.

Instead, do this.

Divide your task into 4 major groupings. There are 4 quarters in the year, so this makes it easy to put the big ideas up front.

Look at the first quarter. There are three months in a quarter, so divide that idea into thirds.

There are 13 weeks in a quarter and roughly 4-5 weeks in a month.

We will now track our goals with monthly targets, while building our plan to fall on a regular week cycle.

Assume we will take a break from the project one day per week. That will be your day of rest.

Work on your project on all the other days of the week. If you only have 3 minutes, spend those three minutes daily. If you can give more time, do it. The SingleThreading Spreadsheet will build your calendar for you:

Six days on, One day off.

Day 1, Plan

Day 2, Research

Day 3, Write, Refine & Edit

Day 4 Finalize, Polish

Day 5 Polish,

Day 6 Publish

Day 7 Rest and Enjoy

Each time you touch the project, you will build a connection. Movement creates vision. If you try to build the entire project only from the ideas of standing in one place, your vision will be limited to that original point in time and place.

Similar to climbing a mountain, if you stay at the bottom and dream of climbing one day, you will lose to the person who takes one step every day. They may take the wrong path, they may reach a dead end and have to backtrack and find another way up. They will probably face challenges of temperature and weather. Rocks and avalanches make the path treacherous, but in the end, they will have valuable experience and then will gain the viewpoint that is only possible from sitting on top of the mountain.

You will still be considering the climb, maybe even buying more gear, while only dreaming of starting the climb. If you had started sooner, you might be finished by now. Start now. Movement is the most important ingredient. Make the plan, adjust the plan, and keep moving.

No plan survives in its original form. Life happens. Feed your experiences back into the plan and make adjustments. Your plan will improve. You will create the next plan faster. The next plan may even be better. Never forget to keep gaining experiences and keep moving.

Update your plan at the end of every month.

But what if you fail? Stephen McCrainie said that "The master has failed more times than the beginner has even tried." Failure teaches us more than success. Do not be afraid to fail. Welcome it. Hurry it along.

The sooner you fail, the sooner you can move to the next attempt. If you procrastinate, fearing failure, you become a slave to the last attempt. You will tell stories about the one failure that ended your dreams. Perhaps you can wax poetic and write songs.

I would prefer to kick you off your butt to go make the next mistake. Hurry along now, don't let the past become an anchor that locks you into mediocrity.

Do not fail to plan.

Ask yourself these questions:

What is the goal of your project?

What are you going to accomplish?

Are there any milestones or deadlines to be met?

What tasks are due on those milestones?

Is there a dependency to be fulfilled?

Does someone else hold the keys to that dependency?

What resources do you need to complete the project and what is the timing?

Are there any gaps in knowledge or information needed to complete each stage?

What is the timing for this knowledge?

Can you learn it or should you outsource?

Write it down, break it down, one day at a time. If this is your One Thing, spend more time doing it.

This is a daily process. Wake up every day and decide to stay on plan for your One Thing.

If you are thinking of doing something, do it NOW. The successful person writes it down and spends as much time every day working on their One Thing.

You should too.

Limit yourself to
doing just ONE THING.

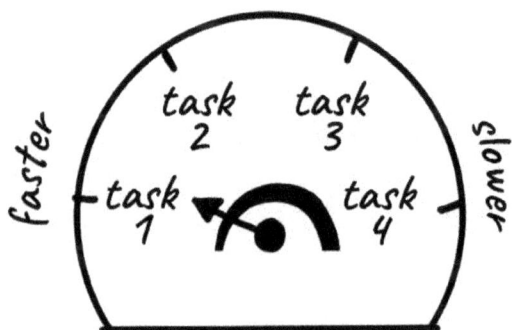

TO-DO-METER

We go faster, learn more deeply,
& produce better results when
we Do One Thing

CHAPTER 12 – BENEFITS OF DOING ONE THING

It ain't what you don't know that gets you into trouble. It's what you know for sure that just ain't so. —Mark Twain

In high school I dreamed of becoming multi-lingual. I signed up for language class to make this dream come true. I took Spanish and switched to Russian after two years. With no increase in ability I switched again and in college started German.

I mistakenly thought that taking all the classes would magically confer an ability to speak those langauges. It did not. I dabbled. I didn't focus.

Today I cannot speak those languages. I can usually differentiate the sound and rhythm of each of these languages. I know a few words. I have no additional ability and I doubted my abilty to learn any language. I thought language was for gifted people.

When the Air Force assigned me to Yokota Air Base

in Japan, I got interested in learning Japanese. My expectations were low. I planned to learn a few words and to eventually recognize the sounds of the language much like I did with other languages.

In preparation for my trip to Japan, I asked for tips and phrases from a college professor. Our schedules allowed for exactly three sessions. I wanted to skip the complicated writing system and go directly to words and greetings.

However, the professor insisted that without learning the written syllabary, it would be worthless to learn words. I would never progress in learning greetings.

Under duress, and with the time limitation, I focused on memorizing 46 hiragana, the simplest form of writing. I did nothing else for the week because I wanted to make the most of the remaining two sessions.

I was SingleThreading. I was not yet aware that I was SingleThreading. I was not yet aware of my abilities to grow.

I thank Yoshida-sensei for insisting that I learn the hiragana. The hiragana and the idea of focusing on one thing at a time became the foundation for my future abilty to learn Japanese and my ability to grow in other areas of my life.

Focusing on One Thing for a specific result started to become a habit. My next challenge to apply SingleThreading was learning how to become a better pilot in the US Air Force.

I wanted to fly as much as possible. That seemed to be the sensible way to progress by having first-hand experience and a lot of flying hours.

Soon I realized that aviation was an unforgiving place. It was better to be thoroughly aquainted with any possible problem that could occur, the possible solutions, and the permissions required to implement those solutions.

I started reading everything that I could find about flying. This included my aircraft manuals, Air Force Regulations and Instructions, and books on aviation accidents.

I learned about the physiology of humans and the ways our body could fool us. I studied the mechanical systems on my plane. I went so far as to find the original engineers to ask about design decisions made to build the plane. I spent time in the maintenace shack learning first-hand about the airplane and the people who kept them flying.

I was SingleThreading my flying career. I didn't know it at the time, but soon I would have a chance to test out my depth of knowledge on the aircraft.

We were fully loaded with passengers on a C-9 medevac mission from Guam to South Korea. It was time to start the engines. Shortly after starting both engines a super loud rattling sound started behind the pilot's head.

There were no warning lights and all systems seemed normal, but the loud rattling was not normal.

The Aircraft commander direced a shut down of the engines and went inside the ops shack to call home for advice.

The squadron commander and the Stan Eval team back at Yokota Air Base had flown this airplane the day prior, experienced a rattling, and maintenance had not found a problem, so we were ordered to start engines and fly the mission.

I refused. Based on my intimate knowledge of the panel behind the pilot's head, the location of the rattling, and the barely observable flickering of one of the lights—and my intution—I belived the rattling noise was coming from the DC bus inverter switch. This is a high amperage system that switches all the important aircraft equipment over to the battery in case of an electrical failure from the engine generators.

The switch itself rarely fails. The sensor that tells the switch which position to flip to could very easily fail. I assumed the signal was at fault causing the switch to become unstable, rapidly moving power from the battery to the generators and back again like a drummer on steroids. A high amperage load was going back and forth and the heat would grow and sparks would fly.

This fault will not illuminate warning lights. There was no procedure in the manual. Nothing in the normal sequence of training or flying experince would identify this malfunction.

As a co-pilot 2nd Lieutenant, I was the lowest officer rank in the chain of people opposing me and demanding that we fly that day. The aircraft commander was a Captain and once again gave me the news that we were to fly that day.

No amount of explanation or reasoning was working so I ripped off my pilot wings from my flight suit and insisted they find another pilot to fly the mission.

On the ground this malfunction was noisy. In flight the results might be disastrous. We could potentially lose all power to the cockpit! Or worse, we could lose the aircraft and the crew and passengers. I was not comfortable flying with a malufunctioning critical component.

We unloaded and waiting for the alternate crew to arrive with our replacment plane from Japan. We would load our passengers on that new plane and continue to Korea.

That crew took jumped into our broken plane, started the engines, and began taxiing to the runway for takeoff. The nose of that plane dipped suddenly as they stopped abruptly and returned to parking. The rattle was indeed a serious problem. It was NOT the one they had assumed on the phone call.

If I had studied my aircraft in the same way I learned Spanish, German, and Russian, I would not have had the conviction to hold firm. It was my depth of knowledge gained from SingleThreading that put me in the position to make a solid decicison.

SingleThreading gave me the conviction to refuse to fly despite being the newest and youngest pilot in the squadron. My expertise was not gained from the number of hours in the pilot's seat. My expertise came from focusing on One Thing.

You do not have to be good at everything you do. You should be good at something. The thing you are good at, you should work hard to become better at doing. Know your one thing from every angle. Be a professional. That is the benefit of focusing on One Thing.

The benefits of SingleThreading become evident the longer you focus on Doing One Thing.

Just Do Your One Thing.

Doing one thing frees you from the tyranny of task switching. You avoid the busyness trap and the fallacy that doing many things will make you productive.

The benefits of doing One Thing are simple. You gain lasting success, retain lifetime ability, reach expertise and expert status faster, and grow a depth of understanding and knowledge that permit you to make better decisions throughout your life.

Before reading this, visualize the benefits of SingleThreading in your own life.

Recall times when you have already achieved depth by focusing on one thing. Know that focusing on one thing neccesarily means you are missing out on something else. This is normal. The opportunity cost of doing one thing means lost opportunities in other things.

When you do many things at once with the hope that one of them will work out, you are never fully engaged in any of them and will not achieve significance in anything.

Stay true to SingleThreading. Work to win benefits more often and win them faster. Do not fear missing other opportunities. Chasing other opportunities before you finish SingleThreading is a false herring.

Intelligence

The time between
new information,
and making a
decision is,
intelligence!

CHAPTER 13 – MOTIVATION

How do you get so much done? By starting.

I get asked all the time, where does my energy and motivation come from? People want to know how they can get to that level of motivation.

I don't have an answer for everyone. Motivation seems to be part of our human nature. The kid who cannot get out of bed on a school day easily wakes up at 5 am to go skiing. Clearly, they are motivated for skiing and not for school.

If you are not motivated to do something that is important, perhaps you need to look at the results that you are seeking. Somewhere in your mind, you are doing these things because you want the result that they bring. So, as Steven Covey says, begin with the end in mind.

Think about the final state you want to achieve and break that down into smaller steps. I recommend the SingleThreading Calendar as a starting point. It is easy to start from the big, delicious finish, and then identify the chunks that bring you to that state.

I remember when I was in High School in White Plains, New York. I was to take the NY State Regents for Math so that I could enter Engineering School. I asked my math teacher how to get a high score on the Regents. He told me to take every Regents Exam for the past 5 years at least 5 times each.

I bought 5 years-worth of the massive study prep-guides with the sample questions. I completed each book, moved on to the next, and continued this process until I had completed every question in every book 5 times. It was a massive undertaking. I spent hours on this every day.

When it came time to take the official exam, I could see the patterns in the questions and the slight differences between the ones I had taken. I knew instinctively which questions I could answer immediately and which needed formulas to solve. I had all the formulas at my fingertips from using them so many times for so many hours.

The test was easy for me and I got a nearly perfect score. I didn't "study" for the test, I took the test over and over with immediate feedback. If you want to get better at something, go out and fail fast. Do it now, and do it again. And again. Build up the reps until it becomes second nature.

Where did I get the "motivation" to do this? I was afraid of failure. I was afraid of what would happen if I could not get into a good school. I believed the advice of my teacher. I began the process by buying the books.

While I studied, I turned off all social events. I made time for this. This focus made all the difference.

I did not enjoy taking tests over and over. I was not "motivated" to do the work—I was afraid of not getting into my college of choice. I feared the loss of an opportunity more than I hated taking the practice tests.

There was no intrinsic motivation, it was a "fear of loss" motivation.

How do you get motivated? Think about what will happen if you do not complete the task sitting before you.

Not everyone is motivated by this aversion to loss. Some people don't care what college they get into. As long as they can get into a safe school, they would prefer not to work as hard. There would be no way to motivate that person to work harder. The drive to avoid the pain of studying is stronger than the pain of not getting into a specific school.

Motivation is personal. It must be important to you for reasons that you define. Know yourself and make the best decisions you can.

CHAPTER 14 – THE RELUCTANCE TO CHANGE

How much time will you give your One Thing?

When we don't hate what we do enough to change, we accept the status quo. Good chance there is a better path just outside of your current life. A worse path is not too far off either. You cannot survive the storms of a poor decision without the conviction that you are going to be better off in the new direction.

Therefore, do not march off without conviction. You must first have belief in yourself and belief in your future. When you feel strongly enough about moving forward that you will burn the bridges behind you to ensure no retreat, now you have enough conviction to succeed.

This conviction may originate in fear, hatred,

sadness, or other strong emotion. If it comes from happiness, I suggest you reconsider. Happiness is fleeting and rarely drives the reluctant person forward. Success comes from experience. Experience comes from Pain. Happiness does not bring success. Success brings happiness.

Put in the work. "Hard work beats talent when talent doesn't work hard." If you are ready to put in the work and if you are ready to go it alone (even when the odds are against you) this might be your calling.

If you can continue working after you have exceeded the requirements, this is probably the path that you should keep working on. If you think deeply about how to complete the project and can "see" the finished project even when it is only an idea, this might be something you can continue working on even when it seems impossible.

Start with a focus on the things that seem easy to you. That way, when it becomes difficult, you can continue without loss of enthusiasm.

If you are not in a position that brings out the tiger in you, you are probably not using your talents effectively.

I wonder why any of us continue to push through in areas where we lack talent. I believe part of the reason is our experience in school. If we got good grades in English and poor grades in History, we were told to work harder in History and English got very little encouragement.

We probably should have learned to work more diligently on our talent in English. Instead, we are pushed to work harder on History.

Through life, we have learned the feeling of working harder to get better. That translates to us learning how to work harder for our boss. It is the best use of your energy for your company, but perhaps not the best use of your talents. It might not be where your comparative advantage lives.

Look at the skills that you find easy. The things that you can't imagine someone paying you to do because they seem too simple. The things that you do, no matter what is happening in your life.

I gave this same discussion to a friend I met at a trade show. He was 50% owner of a magazine that covered aviation topics. He was at every aviation related trade show worldwide gathering insights and publishing his stories. He was a prolific writer, and the magazine had been in his family since his father started it. He and his brother were the sole owners, and the business was great!

But he hated it. He was almost 60 years old and felt like he was wasting his life. I asked what he wanted to do, and he told me it was too silly. He didn't think it would succeed and so it was only a pipe dream.

When he said those words, there was a twinkle in his eye. A spark he didn't have when talking about the aviation magazine.

I told him the story of a lady I met at the Delta Skymiles Lounge in Seattle. She was a single mother with 4 kids in New York. Her husband died, leaving her with no income and no way to feed the kids.

So, she started a physical, printed newspaper when readership everywhere on printed content was down. She did not write for the entire country or the entire state. She wrote a newspaper for a single building. She interviewed people and shared their stories.

It turns out that people are very interested in local news.

That single paper turned into multiple papers for all the nearby buildings. Then it grew and grew until she became a local news leader. She is fairly wealthy now because she focused on things that were right in front of her.

When I told my friend these stories, he opened up to me. He actually wanted to do the same. He was from a small town in New York and wanted to start a little magazine about things local to the town.

I forgot about our conversation until he called me a year later. He did it. He gave his magazine a fun name and launched to raving fans who were eager for this type of local news.

It was an instant success. He said the moment he heard about the succesful print business was the moment he decided to commit.

That one story changed his life in that one moment. He sold his share of the aviation magazine and started the new venture focused on a single town.

He developed readers all over the world in a short time. Locals who had moved abroad. Tourists eager to learn more for their visit.

He found his acre of diamonds.

I hope you too find yours. It is in you somewhere. You only have to look to find it.

CHAPTER 15 – THE FOOD WE CONSUME

"The food you eat can be either the safest and most powerful form of medicine or the slowest form of poison." — Ann Wigmore

Eat Real Food

Real Food =

AVOID Sugar
Fat Free
Processed Foods
High Fructose Corn Syrup

We all want to be healthy. If there was a simple, easy, one-size-fits-all approach, we would probably do it. In fact, there might be a simple way, but it might be hidden from us.

Hidden doesn't mean we cannot see it. Hidden means we have been conditioned to think and eat in ways that are not healthy. Like the needles in a stack of needles, it is in front of us, but we cannot see it.

Like SingleThreading, the idea of a better diet is probably so simple, you will wonder why you have not tried it before.

Consider your own circumstances. Look at your energy levels. How does it feel to think? If your energy level is low and you despise thinking; if you feel stressed often, you might not have read this far. But if you are here and wondering about those low energy moments, don't jump for a coffee or an energy drink. Look at your diet.

If you are planning to start SingleThreading, you want your brain ready and able to accept new challenges. Give your brain the energy it deserves.

Although the brain is powered by sugars, (specifically glucose) you must avoid high fructose corn syrup. This is not the same as glucose! Look for fresh fruits such as blueberries and blackberries (Darker fruits are typical excellent brain food).

What else does the brain and body need? Here is where it gets murky.

In 1943, the world was in crises and food was scarce. The US Government tried to help people figure out what foods they could skip and still function. So they gave us the Basic Food Guide.

Later, in 1980, the US Government told us that consuming fat makes us fat. This came from an earlier study (paid for by the Sugar Research Foundation) that linked fat consumption to heart disease. A study that got people to shun fat and consume more sugar. Because if you can get people to eat less fat, they will replace that missing flavor with something—sugar. Manufacturers raced to make fat-free and low-fat products.

Although that study was ultimately proved as flawed, it was a big win for the sugar producers. It still is a winning business strategy based on the shelves at your supermarket. They convinced people to eat less

SINGLETHREADING – Just Do One Thing

fat, replace that fat with sugar, and make it sound healthy. Even though that study was completely skewed, we still cling to the empty promise of fat-free products.

How was the study flawed?

The study linked fat in the body to increased incidence of heart failure. Good, so far. They then noticed that people who ate fat in the study had fat in their body. And then they jumped the shark and said eating fat makes heart disease more likely.

The study ignored places like France and Okinawa that ate a lot of fat in their diet yet had low incidences of heart failure.

It turns out the participants were gaining fat from the sugar they ate, not the fat in their food. The fat they ate was not causal to the fat in their arteries—the sugar was. We need fat in our diet not sugar.

Eating fat does not automatically convert to fat in your body. Our body is a chemical factory that takes in sugars and converts the sugars to fat.

Further, fat on your body is not necessarily a bad thing. Your brain is soggy wet bag that is 60% made of fat. Fat is an amazing, compact source of energy. When you go long stretches without food, this source of energy can mean the difference between survival and perishing. 1 kg of fat contains 7,700 kcal of energy.

A typical person requires between 2,000-2,500 kcal of energy to maintain a normal healthy body. 1.82–2.27 kg of body fat could in theory provide power to the body for 7 days. (You still need water to extract the energy.)

So if added sugar is bad for us, how did we get to the place where we consume more sugars than our body requires? Why did sugar and other chemicals become standard replacemetns for fat?

It starts with our body's desire for things that are sweet. When fat is removed taste is also removed. Replacing it with sweetener does the trick. So suagar and other flavor chemicals were added.

Without the fat your body does not send the signal

to stop eating. You do not get the feeling of being full. So you eat more than you normally would.

Producers sell more sugar, we eat more and more of their concoctions, and they make more money. Triple play. Companies use sugar and sweetner substitutes as the signal to make something more desirable—ensuring we buy more from them.

Did you know? When they remove the fat from a product, they can use the fat to make creams and butter to make more profits again!

And you eat more. And when you eat more, and more of what you eat contains sugars, then you help increase the profits of companies selling you these items. And you gain weight, while slowly killing your body. There is no incentive for companies to change the compound!

If they provided healthier choices you would eat less and they would make less profits. It is up to you to make healthier choices. You have access to all the information.

Replacing fat with sugar is no longer sufficient. The food manufacturers have developed ultra processed food to help us consume more.

To be fair, all humans have been processing food for as long as we have had fire. Unlike animals in the wild, our human bodies require many of our foods to be partially processed before we conusme them. Chopping, grinding, fermenting, heating, mixing and combining are all part of our external processing steps. For centuries, this has been done in kitchens all over the world. All good so far.

Food manufacturers learned that they could remove fat and replace it with sugar. People ate more and sales increased. Subsequently, sugar was demonized. So manufacturers put time, energy, and resources into enegineering food better. This ultraprocessed food is consumed faster, and you can eat more of it before feeling full. This new food speeds up intake, increases absorption, and provides increased sales.

The by product of people being able to eat more and eat more quickly is our current obesity pandemic.

This is why I say the answer to improved health is invisible, yet right in front of you. But might be looking at the wrong thing.

My guess is that you are not getting the full complement of nutrients that your body requires to be at its best. When you lack the required nutrients, your body will continually seek more. A bowl of ice cream feels good because "more food" is the body's first attempt to gain "more nutrients." If you could get the right combination of nutrients, you would eat less. In our fast-paced world, it is difficult to get every nutrient that you need from a typical diet.

You are checking the fat content when you should check the sugar! (Fake sugar is not the answer). Eat the fat, shun the sugar.

You are consuming ultra processed foods that create inflamation throughout your body. This geenrates many of the inflamtory related diseases.

How bad is this increased sugar, ultraprocessed food, and fat free situation? I love a little yogurt in the morning. But I always disliked the taste of yogurt. Or so I thought. It turns out I was eating the chemically induced flavors that are so popular in the US. On a shelf filled with yogurts, most of them were no or low fat, using a long list of chemicals to make up for the loss in flavor.

My sensitive tongue was picking up the artificial chemical flavors of those fillers. Now, I eat yogurt that says 100% milk. Nothing else. No flavors and no chemicals. Always go for the full fat yogurt if you want to stay healthy. Same for milk. (In the US, try to find the milk that does not have hormones added though).

On a typical supermarket shelf, there is only one or two full-fat, 100% whole milk, non-flavored yogurt(s). You have to look carefully and read a lot of labels to find them.

You need the fat in the food to give you a full feeling. You need fat in the food for your brain to function properly. Specifically, non-saturated omega-3 fats.

We are still learning about the brain-gut link, but the results say eat healthy fat! Before I knew about this,

I was still following the US Government guidance.

Remember the food pyramid from 1992? That chart started off as a good idea but was tampered with by people who profit from what you eat. The food pyramid showed 6-11 servings of bread, cereal, rice, and pasta. I like the foods listed. I cannot imagine a day when I could eat 11 complete servings. But when I tried to reach this standard, my weight reached 100 kg (220 lbs).

I cannot imagine going back to that many servings of bread each day. I reached that impressive weight with a normal 6-11 servings of bread and pasta plus the other things on the pyramid.

I'm not saying you shouldn't eat bread and pasta, but eleven servings a day will give you a larger body. All those carbohydrates convert in your body's chemical factory to become fat that is stored for a rainy day when the food supply dwindles. If the supply never dwindles and if you have this many servings daily, you will continue to get heavier.

That food pyramid was flawed on the day it was

published. The nutrition experts who consulted on the product were exasperated to see their work mangled to make a whole separate group for milk and increased portions for bread. Serving sizes increased. The voices of nutrition experts were drowned out by the profit industry.

Back to sugar. To this day, Americans eat a lot more sugar today than we should. After reviewing 100s of journals and studies, I recommend that your sugar intake not exceed 5% of your calories. In terms of quantity, that's less than 30g of sugar per day.

For most of human existence, we did not consume any reasonable quantity of sugar at all. In 1700, the average person consumed less than 5 g of sugar per day. By 1900, that number was up to 112 g per day. Why? Better access to sugar. Because the slave trade from Africa to the Caribbean and the Americas allowed the relatively inexpensive processing of sugar cane (not counting the human loss).

That brutal work required a constant influx of new labor to meet the growing demand, thus the continuing of the slave trade. Ruining your own body to eat sugar while ruining the lives of entire generations of people. Ugh.

We kept eating the sugar. We started drinking sodas with every meal. We added sugars to our tea and coffee. And then sugar was on a roll. It was in everything from donuts to our table salt (helped keep the salt from clumping).

Today, we know the increased sugars in your body cause a spike in insulin driving the diabetes epidemic. And the diabetes epidemic is not waning. We can't stop eating sugar. Fake sugar and sweetners do not provide better health!

You should look carefully at the information on the labels. Remember you are feeding your brain. Cut back on added sugars and sweeteners.

Eat fresh fruits, vegetables, omega-3 non-saturated fats, protiens and minerals and appropriate level of carbohydrates so that your body and your mind can thrive.

If you count your calories, be sure to pay attention to the source of the calories. All calories are not equally beneficial to the body.

Removing the fat and replacing it with chemicals to add back the flavor is killing you slowly, causing you to feel you never get enough food, so you eat more, and it is degrading the power of your brain.

Avoid the sugar. Check that healthy granola bar. There are 8 - 15g of sugar in there. Not a problem if you are eating a healthy diet and that's your once in a blue-moon snack. But if this is a daily munchable, look out, you are feeding a sugar high.

When you are in the supermarket, notice that the processed food sits in the middle of the store. Fresh food is almost always situated around the perimeter of the store. Shop from the outside. Avoid the middle of the store.

If you like to drink smoothies as the way to consume your fruits, be sure to measure the calories. All smoothies are not created equal. If you buy store-bought or pre-mixed, good chance the smoothies are high in sugars and calories. If you add those calories and that sugar to a regular diet, you might be exceeding the calories you need in a day. More calories in that you expend will mean you store fat. Do that every day @ 500 kcal and in one year you will have gained over 20 kg. That's probably how I got to 100 kg from my nominal weight of 83 kg.

Eat with care. Reduce the potato intake and increase the green vegetable intake. Eat the whole broccoli, not the smoothie. Eat the fruit with the fibers, reduce the smoothie. Eat eggs. Eat the fat on the bacon and your steak. (Don't eat to excess, but don't cut it all off). Cut out refined foods like white sugar, refined grains in white bread, and any place you find refined grains. Eat whole grains if you can. Use healthy oils (olive oil is great). Drink water.

Read those labels, measure those calories. You do not have to do it every time you shop. Look at where you are today. Look in your cabinets. Record what you eat for 7 days.

All calories are not created equally. You need a

balance of nutrition in your diet. You would not want to live entirely on sugar for your calories since it lacks the proteins, fats, and minerals you need to keep your body functioning.

Try a week. Keep a notebook to track your calories and exercise. Don't try to remember. Write it down as soon as you eat. Weigh the food if you can for more precise measurements. (Or use an app to track your food). See what you are eating.

When I tried this, I took notes at the end of the day trying to recall all that I ate. I added up the numbers and was eating 1800 kcal a day while gaining weight. It didn't make sense.

Then I started recording food as I ate it. It turns out I was grazing in between meals and by the time I wrote it all down, my brain conveniently forgot about those snacks. Healthy snacks like nuts and raisins, a café latte or two. But the actual caloric intake was over 2700 kcal. I was off by over 900 kcal a day! No wonder I was gaining fast.

I am not the expert in nutrition. To my surprise,

most medical doctors are also only minimally trained in nutrition. Unless you are interested in this field, it remains something of an outlier. This means we end up eating things that are advertised to us, have bright colors, and are easy to purchase.

My goal is not to attempt a full explanation in one chapter. I want to plant the seed that you should make a change. It will take some time and energy, but it will be worth it.

I am asking you to work to make your diet healthier by using real food. Become a food critic. Critique your own food.

There is no one perfect diet. But there is surely one terrible diet. That is the diet that avoids fat, eats refined grains and refined sugars, and takes in high fructose corn syrup along with a host of other fake sugars to be "healthy."

It probably costs less than eating healthy. You are going to pay in health care costs.

Our healthcare system is designed to take care of sick people. I want you to avoid the system and stay healthy.

Fix your food first.

CHAPTER 16 – EXERCISE & MEDITATION

You should treat your mind no differently than your body. You have to train both.
—Arnold Schwarzenegger

When we think about exercise, most of us think about "going to the gym." We have lost the idea that exercise can happen without a formal setting.

I want you to consider ways to incorporate exercise in your normal day. If you can make time for the gym, Go for it!

For those who sign up for the gym membership but never actually go; for those who live too far from the gym; or if you just dislike going to the gym—but you want to be healthy and you want to exercise but are not sure what to do:

Remember that your body is a system of systems. The foot bone is connected to the leg bone and so on. All of your bones are connected to tendons and muscles.

When we use the muscles to failure, the body sends a signal to increase the muscle density in that area. If you don't use them, the body pulls cells away and they atrophy.

When you do not exceed a certain range of motion, the body lets the tendons and muscles reduce their length to fit the expected range of motion.

Your entire body is an anticipation machine. It anticipates how much you move in a day and burns that amount of calories from local stores. If you move more, you will burn more calories. The body will plan ahead and attempt to consume those calories.

For this system to work, you must work out on a regular schedule. At least once a day or every other day. Your body loves consistency.

The key is to do something every day. Consider all the muscle groups. Look up calisthenics and other exercises that use only your body weight. Look at stretch routines on YouTube. Find a pattern that works for you. The information you need is available if you go looking for it. You can even hire a coach online or find a series of workouts tailored to fit you. Check out yoga for a combination of stretching and calisthenics.

We think about food and exercise. But since we are all slightly different in our body type and medical history, there is no one perfect diet or exercise regime that works for everyone.

Discover what works and what doesn't work for you.

One of the simplest and most effective ways to exercise is to include walking in your daily routine. You can walk any time of day, anywhere, inside or outside and doesn't require specialized equipment or clothing. For me, one of the biggest benefits is that I don't sweat profusely when I walk, but I do when I run. When I run, there is no possibility of stopping off for an errand along the way. I would make a mess of the floor as I dripped sweat. No such difficulties with walking.

Walking for at least 30 minutes a day has amazing benefits to include improved mood, lowered risk of heart disease and stroke, increased energy levels and overall fitness improvement. I started at walking for 30 minutes and eventually got up to 90 minutes a day. My bone density increased 30% and my memory seemed better.

How is all of this possible?

On the brain front alone, researchers have discovered that each step boosts a powerful wave of oxygenated blood into the brain. Kind of like clearing out the cobwebs.

When you walk, you bring benefits to flexibility, range of motion and help prevent injury.

Stretching is also an important component of a daily health routine. Every time I stretch, I get a little better flexibility. As I grow older, I wish I had started stretching sooner. Especially ankles and wrists. Learning how to fall gracefully while improving range of motion to help prevent injury. Experts recommend stretching for at least 10-15 minutes per day, focusing on all major muscle groups. I love this idea! But if you cannot fit in a 30 minute or even a 15 minute workout, start with a 5 minute workout. Some is better than none.

In terms of when to exercise, I fit in my routines throughout the day. I know there are some people who like to start their day with a workout. Others who like to work out after the workday is done.

The morning crowd says the work out gets their metabolism going and allows their energy level to rise. The after work crowd says they can relax and unwind after a long day.

The time other people work out is not important. Finding a time that works for you is important. Build an exercise schedule in advance and treat it as a non-negotiable appointment with yourself. Give your body the priority it needs to keep the rest of you functioning.

SINGLETHREADING – Just Do One Thing

Take a lunchtime walk around your office. Wait until you get home to decompress. Do your best to find a variety of exercises so that you don't work the same muscle groups all the time. Vary your walking speed from slow to quick. Join a group or create your own workout partner. Make a mix tape for your workout if you cannot find a partner. The music will keep you on track. I use YouTube for my workout music, since Spotify only allows random music.

Stretching, walking, and strength training should be the core of your daily workout routine.

In addition to exercise and stretching, make time to work on your mind.

Use meditation. I think we fail to recognize this powerful technique for better sleep, better decision making, and for better healthier living.

Meditation is another powerful tool for managing our brains. Through regular meditation practice, we can train our minds to be more focused and resilient and better able to manage stress.

Research says that meditation can improve cognitive function and even reduce anxiety. I know it gives me a feeling of power in my mind. That is a state of well-being that I appreciate any time I am working.

Meditation is a way of giving the brain a pause. Resetting our thinking so that we can gear up for another shot.

In a study regarding the benefits of mindfulness training, researchers discovered a noticeable growth in the frontal lobes of all the study participants after 7 hours.

You can start with just seconds a day. Feel stressed? Perform a tiny spot meditation. Instead of picking up your phone, focus on your breath...in...out... really focus and imagine it going in your lungs, exchanging the molecules in your lungs and coming back out.

Do this for 3 minutes 5 times a day. 15 minutes a day. You could also do 5 minutes 3 times a day. Try it at mealtimes. Find the pattern that works for you. You can do this anywhere.

(The 3x5 system in Appendix 1 works for nearly everything).

In 28 days, you will experience 7 hours of mindfulness training, feeling better and stronger. Keep it up for the rest of the year and change your life!

These moments will return the feeling of control to you. You will wonder why you didn't start sooner. You will feel powerful again.

There are many kinds of meditation and I cannot tell you all about them in a small chapter in a book on SingleThreading, so I will tell you what I think meditation is.

The simplest and most powerful method of meditation involves focusing on your body. I like to use my breathing as the focus. I imagine I can follow a molecule of air as it enters my lips or nose, travels down into my lungs, then through my blood, and back out as carbon dioxide. I do this for three full breaths.

As I am still a neophyte in this process, if I am outside or in my office, I stop after 3-5 breaths. I find that I start forgetting how to breathe! Sounds silly, but the intense focus on such an obvious task makes me conscious of the fact that I've never been conscious of my breath before. This wonderment drives me to control my breathing manually, and I do not know how to do that. It seems so simple, and yet there is are so many steps involved.

But while I am managing my breathing, my brain is focused entirely on this one task. And I am giving my brain a break from all the other tasks weighing upon it.

When I come out of my mini meditation, I feel more awake and more alert.

In addition to mindfulness meditation, I want to give a pitch for forgiveness. Again, strange to have this here in the chapter on exercise, but I think they are connected. When you work out, your brain wanders to various subjects. Or at least my mind does.

Sometimes it invents scenarios or recalls times when someone hurt me or I was callous to someone.

I take those moments to forgive completely. If I need to reach out to them, I make a note to do it right away. The key is to clear my mind of clutter that might slow it down. Having random thoughts stuck in the mind will drag your whole day and limit your ability to perform SingleThreading. So, if you get one of these workout thoughts, write it down and get back to your workout.

Take care of those thoughts so they never have to intrude on your workout again.

Keep a daily workout routine, eliminate thoughts that linger, and generate energy to do your One Thing.

Digging into the mind and learning how the ancient traditions and techniques can work for us today is mind blowing.

CHAPTER 17 – REST

So, to prevent fatigue and worry, the first rule is:
Rest often. Rest before you get tired.
—Dale Carnegie

D ale Carnegie wrote a book titled "How to Win Friends and Influence People." He said that we should rest before we get tired.

That is a great way to think about how sleep affects our ability to perform. Resting gives us energy to do more.

I used to be very good at the standing long jump. I was not in track and field; I rode a unicycle every day. It turns out that is the perfect exercise for improving your long jump.

During leadership training one day, there was a long jump competition. It was included in a session on stepping out of our comfort zone. I don't recall how it started, but I remember the outcome.

Participants jumped three times and would record the best of three. I gave my everything to my first jump. It was the winning jump and the longest for everyone in the competition. But since I had gone so far, everyone was excited to see make the next two jumps as well.

Those next two jumps fell way short of the first jump. Not even close. I had no more energy after crushing the first jump. But instead of feeling great about the first jump, I felt bad about not showing improvement. What happened?

I did not recover after the first jump. No rest.

This is the same in life. Some days, I stay up late or even stay up all night to finish projects. I thought it had no ill effects. I didn't drink coffee, but also did not get sleepy. After three or four nights of limited or no sleep, it became difficult to stay awake in daytime meetings. This was the cumulative effect of not sleeping.

Now I treat my body much better than I did in those younger days. I work hard to get enough sleep. I make plans to sleep on time and then to wake up early. The shift in my cognitive ability is significant. The right food, the right amount of exercise and the right amount of sleep make all the difference.

In the Air Force, we learned to operate on limited amounts of sleep. But we also learned that if you didn't get sleep that your body needed, your body would steal that sleep from you—usually at the worst possible time.

Pilots on short final, the last few minutes of the flight before touchdown and landing, need to be at their most vigilant. Yet if they are sleepy, that is when they were most likely to experience micro-sleep—limited cognitive gaps where they appear to be awake, with their eyes open, but their brain is unable to process details at a conscious level. They are effectively sleeping with their eyes open.

To avoid this dangerous micro-sleep, the Air Force taught me to take brief naps. Through time, I discovered my ideal nap is 45 minutes long, or any multiple of 45 minutes. I feel groggy after a 10 or

20 minute nap, but fully energized after a 45 minute nap. I feel more alert after a 90 minute nap than a 2 hour nap.

Other people I have spoken to respond well to 5-minute or 20-minute naps. Get to know your nap number and give it a try.

Sleep, for most of us, is not optional. Studies have shown that a better quality of sleep leads to improved concentration and improved decision making. The two things we want for our SingleThreading life.

Other notable benefits include improved immune system, better metabolism, increased short-term and long-term memory, and a long list of other vital function improvements.

However, so many of us get suboptimal sleep. If you are one of those, look at your pre-bedtime ritual.

Some easy to spot culprits include afternoon coffee or tea. That caffeine can stick around for 12 or more hours. Even if you have not observed the effects before, it's likely you didn't *notice* the effects.

Chapter 17 – Rest

Listen carefully to your body and avoid those late afternoon lattes.

What about those TV/Phone/PC habits we all have before bed? Have you been spending your last minutes before bedtime with your laptop, PC, phone, or tablet? The blue light from those devices tells your brain that it is still daytime. And that can disrupt your sleep rhythm. Maybe try a paper book before bed to wean yourself from your many screens.

Give yourself a full body stretch or massage your head and temples. Soothing stretches and massages help relax your body to enter sleep mode.

When in bed, lights out for best results. Some people can sleep with lights on, but most find they have better sleep when it is completely dark.

Do not mix your sleeping space with work. Your body has a loci memory for places. If you often do work or watch movies in bed, that is what the body will expect. Turn off the TV and separate the bed for sleeping and only sleeping. Just like training a new puppy, eventually, your brain will get the hint.

Finally, set a regular bedtime and work towards keeping it. Pair that with a reasonable time to wake up and build this as an impenetrable time. Nothing shall interfere with this time. Turn off all notifications on your phone and give yourself the protected time to sleep.

The benefits of good sleep far outweigh the negatives of trying to work on a little sleep. Yes, it is possible to function on a little sleep, but it is not ideal. Give your body the recovery it needs. Sleep.

Sleep is critical
Meditate Too!

Rest Before
You Get Tired

Forgive, Listen
Be Thankful

Refresh, Recharge, Balance

CHAPTER 18 – STAYING CLEAN

The objective of cleaning is not just to clean, but to feel happiness living within that environment.
—Marie Kondo

You might wonder, in all this SingleThreading conversation, is there any time to keep your living space tidy and organized.

Maybe you can stay organized and clean for temporary bouts of time, but over time, entropy takes over and before you know it, your sink is full of dishes, some trash cans never get emptied, and clutter seems to appear on every surface.

You know life was meant to be better than this, but you are busy. What can be done?

I struggled with this too. Now I have a few shortcuts that really help. I call them shortcuts because they save me time, but hopefully I am not skipping important steps.

Find out which one works best so that you can spend more time SingleThreading.

The world is built on entropy: a gradual decline into disorder. Entropy happens slowly over time. It is inevitable. Dust appears. Dirty dishes accumulate. If you clean as you go, you balance the entropy. Wait until later to clean, and it takes increased energy to clean up.

It takes energy to keep a room organized because of entropy. It is easier to spend small bits of energy throughout the day than it is to spend a large cache of energy one day a week.

It is the same process for learning a language or developing a workout. Small bits of energy daily provide the best results.

For example: clean the shower while taking a shower. Clean the toilet on a weekly schedule. Declutter your desk each time you change projects. Move the previous project to a cubby while the new project takes center stage.

For the kitchen sink, what if everyone in the house had exactly one plate, one bowl, one cup, one fork, one spoon, and one knife. When that one item is in the sink, they have to wash it to for their next meal.

If you live alone, this will force you to clean in small increments throughout the day. Do you wash dishes every night before bed? Then you will never wake up to a sink full of dishes.

Combine exercise and cleaning by using a Swiffer or vacuum to clean up your living space every day.

Clean and polish your shoes every time you get home or once a week (at a minimum).

Check your physical mail daily, but perhaps open them during two days of the month, like the 1st and the 15th.

There are more techniques you can use. One of my favorite is quitting.

Quit using things you can do without. My first challenge was to eliminate trash cans that were all over the house. I found that on trash day I spent a ton of time walking around collecting trash from multiple spots.

Now I have the absolute minimum number of trash cans. Instead of 7, I have 2. I stopped living on carpeted spaces so now I don't have to vacuum, I can use a Swiffer instead. I got rid of paper bills so I no longer have to track the paper. I quit doing things that did not add value.

This is a daily challenge. I do not wait for declutter day. I declutter daily.

Old clothing gets dropped into a box by the door. When the box is full, off to the donation center. Now I have less to clean.

Scissors and pens are always in need. I have one pair of scissors in the kitchen and one near the printer. I do not allow the scissors to wander or take up residence anyplace else—they get put back immediately after use. I eliminated storage containers and got rid of extra junk. Instead of drawers full of stuff, I have two pairs of scissors, one pen, one magic marker, and a notepad. They have only one spot. Clean. Simple. Easy.

I added two under counter storage units for my papers that I need quck access to (less than 30 days). I toss them when finished.

Everything else gets a small space. No rental storage units, no garage space. If it is not in use, it gets recycled. If it is going to be used, it gets a storage space. Nothing is allowed to live on a surface. No table collections.

I do not want to tell you how to live. These are simply ideas for better living. Research shows that there are significant benefits to decluttering and enjoying the minimalism lifestyle.

If you need some more ideas for decluttering, Marie Kondo popularized the KonMari. She wrote a book called "The Life-Changing Magic of Tidying Up." That's the convoluted translation from the original Japanese title. I think the title sounds better in the original Japanese, but the concept is identical. Marie says you should go through your belongings one category at a time (like clothing, books, papers, dishes, etc.) and keep only the items that "spark joy." By keeping only the things that are meaningful, we can let go of the items that are slowing us down and holding us back.

There is also a Four-Box Method. This is labeling four boxes as "trash," "donate," "keep," and "relocate." As you methodically go through your belongings, you put the things you find in one of the boxes. I like this method, although, relocate is ambiguous. I would prefer you use the three boxes and eliminate the relocate box.

The Minimalist Method is to intentionally downscale and focus on living with less. It has the benefit of helping you live below your means. You let go of the things that are extra in your life. Maybe it means moving into a smaller apartment or emptying a monthly storage facility. If you have multiple cars but only drive one, you let the other car go. It could also mean not attending as many social events or choosing a lower class of travel.

One of my favorites is the 10-Minute Method. You

set a timer for 10 minutes and clean for that amount of time. When the timer goes off, you go back to your normal routine. Do this several times in a cleaning day, or once a day on non-cleaning days. You will find the right rhythm for your lifestyle.

A less aggressive way to reduce clutter is the 30-day decluttering challenge. You pick one area, one room, or one spot to declutter. Every day you remove one item from the area for the 30 days. This allows your brain to experience less stress over the idea of having to clean up a large area. It breaks the experience down into small, manageable chunks.

But what if there was less to clean? If you can avoid making a mess in the first place, you do not have to spend time cleaning. When I cook bacon, I place aluminum foil on the pan so there is less to clean. I don't eat crumbly food in my car, so no need to clean up the crumbs.

When my kids were young, we did not have juice, colas, or other sweet drinks in the car. So if there were any spills, there were no sticky spills.

I want to help you stay clean and stay focused. Less energy spent on cleaning means more energy to spend on SingleThreading!

Do MORE with LESS

Throw away before you organize

Organize & Clean your:

house
office
car
applicances
...

CHAPTER 19 – HELPING OTHERS

*Those who are happiest are those who
do the most for others. —Booker T. Washington*

This book started because of the realization that when we do things for ourselves, the results are limited to ourselves. A result with the solution for one person.

What's the point of doing something big if it only helps one person? Isn't it better to spread good ideas? What is the point of working hard on anything if you are not helping others?

If we discover a better way to live or if we find something that will benefit others, we are being selfish if we do not share our insights.

When we share our ideas with the world, we help move the needle in a way that sitting in a room alone by ourselves could never accomplish. We can never fully understand our influence on another person, but it is up to us to make the world a better place with our good ideas.

Our eyes can only look outward. We can never truly look back at ourselves. We rely on others around us to tell us how we impact the world. There are lots of benefits to helping others succeed. We can share insights, be a coach, be a workout partner, help build goals, be a muse, be a sounding board, show interest, or just listen to those around us. Pick someone and be one of these things for them.

You get a feeling of satisfaction that you helped someone. You make an impact and benefit another life. That person can move forward and help someone else. Give a compliment. Ask people to pay it forward.

Working with others can improve performance and give you and your collaborator more motivation to succeed in your separate goals.

My dad and I used to have strange conversations. I would talk about my problems at school. He would talk about his programming troubles with his code. Neither really understood the other's concerns, but we acted interested and then responded from our own perspective on our own problems.

Collaboratively, we solved the problems we brought to the conversation. Not because we got an answer, but because we opened up about our ideas without restricting the other. Something about working and sharing with another person makes the ideas grow in the right direction to a clean finish.

This book is my heartfelt attempt to share ideas with you. Maybe you will find a completely fresh approach and pieces of the puzzle continue to fall into place to make the world a better place.

The Journal of Applied Psychology found that teams that were coached by their peers showed improvement in performance. Becoming a coach also leads to your own personal growth. I am convinced that helping others is always a better path. It helps us both.

Reach out and offer to help. Those who do will

be better off for it. It really works, but there is a caution: know your audience.

I was at Barnes and Noble last week, having a latte. I got a $1 off coupon with my purchase and did not want it to go to waste.

I approached people who looked like college students at the tables studying. They did not want the coupon. I tried another table. Same result. Seven tables and 10 people later, still no takers. I asked if anyone wanted a dollar and people started ignoring me. They wouldn't look up when I approached. I was the weird guy with a weird offer.

Then it hit me. I was talking to the wrong people. These people already had their drink and no plan to buy another. They probably all received a coupon too that they didn't know what to do with. I was trying to pitch my idea to people who were not my target audience.

I turned around and saw people in line about to purchase their drinks.

Chapter 19 – Helping Others

I offered the coupon to the person about to order. She was ecstatic. She was about to purchase the coffee and this coupon would save her a dollar right now!

She even thanked me profusely.

The key to offering help is to make sure you are approaching the right audience. If they refuse you, do not push. Be happy that you got a quick no. Move on and find the person who is eager to give you a quick yes. That's your audience.

Keep looking until you find your audience. They are out there waiting eagerly for your offer.

In closing, I hope my words helped.

What did I miss? What could I do better?

I would love to hear from you. What's one thing that helped you?

My email address is on the last page of this book.

Chat with me. Together let's take SingleThreading to the next level.

3x5 System™

Learn Something

5 minutes

Focus on One Thing

3x a day

5 /minutes

APPENDIX 1 – 3X5 SYSTEM

Have a bias toward action - let's see something happen now. You can break that big plan into small steps and take the first step right away.
—Indira Gandhi

One of the most important things to consider when implementing the SingleThreading concept, starting a new workout routine, or learning a new language, is that you will naturally resist change.

Your friends, family, loved ones, co-workers, (someone) will not be happy that you are trying to change. They will want to spend more time with you or even tell you that your plan or dream is not achievable.

People who have not achieved anything will stop you before you try. People who have achieved great things will not encourage you to try because they know how difficult the road ahead will be. They do not want to be blamed for sending you down a path filled with regret and pain.

The only person you can really count on to support you is yourself or your SingleThreading community.

We know you are changing. So are we. Our common passion is to find a new world within ourselves. Just like my father and I talking past each other, yet finding support in those moments. Let's share ideas and find the energy to continue on our journey. That is more than half the battle.

The other half of the battle is finding the time to make the change!

No matter how busy or stressed you are, nearly everyone can dedicate 3 minutes to work on making a change. It is not a lot of time in the course of a day. Most people still eat three meals a day, so tying those ideas together, I developed the 3x5 system.

It encourages you to spend 3 minutes making a change, learning a new skill, or practicing your art.

Take that 3 minutes and repeat it 5 times a day.

Appendix 1 – 3x5 System

I suggest you can do this right after you eat breakfast, lunch, a snack at 3 pm and dinner. Then one more time before bed. That's 15 minutes per day.

Spread over 365 days (no days off) results in 5,475 minutes or approximately 91 hours invested.

If you cannot manage 3 minutes 5 times a day, how about 5 minutes 3 times a day? If that doesn't work, 15 minutes once a day.

The specifics are not important. Continual practice every day without taking a break is the key.

The Japanese have a saying that you become powerful by continuing. Keizoku wa chikara nari. 継続は力なり.I believe it is easy to start. It is also easy to quit. Only the committed will continue.

I designed the 3x5 system to help people learn Japanese. I expanded it to help people learn English. Today, I realize that those two uses are really a tiny sample of what is possible with the 3x5 system.

You can use this to change your life!

INDEX

INDEX

Recommended Books for further reading:

- Eat that Frog, Brian Tracy
- How to Win Friends and Influence People, Dale Carnegie
- The One Thing, Gary W. Keller and Jay Papasan
- Who Stole My Cheese?, Spencer Johnson
- Acres of Diamonds, Russell Conwell
- The 7 Habits of Highly Effective People, Steven Covey
- Atomic Habits, James Clear
- The Life Changing Magic of Tidying Up, Mari Kondo

INDEX

Notes:

SINGLETHREADING – Just Do One Thing

Thank you.

dylan.monaghan@gmail.com